TROUBLED WATERS

By the same author

Still Waters: Mystery Tales of the Canals

TROUBLED WATERS
Memoirs of a Canal Boatwoman

by

Margaret Cornish

B

M & M BALDWIN
Cleobury Mortimer, Shropshire
2003

First paperback edition June 1994
Reprinted July 2003

ISBN 0 947712 25 9

Cover designed by David Miller.

Published by M & M Baldwin
24 High Street, Cleobury Mortimer,
Kidderminster DY14 8BY, England

email: canals@mbaldwin.free-online.co.uk

Printed by Franklyn Publicity Ltd
Park House, Hurdsfield Road,
Macclesfield SK10 1LL, England

Contents

List of Illustrations

PICTURE CREDITS
Daphne French: 1, 3–4, 10, 13; *Waterways World*: 6; British Waterways Board: 8, 11, 16. Chapter heading illustrations are taken from *Narrowboat Decoration* published by the BCNS.

Dedicated to
DAPHNE

Acknowledgements

To Daphne French, one of the two trainers of war-time women trainees on the Grand Union Canal, who has kindly read the script and approved of the many references to herself.

To Virginia, who also features in much of this reconstruction of our working lives together on the boats.

To Helen, the third member of our crew, and a valued ally.

To Bob Shopland, editor of *Waterways World*, who started me off on writing up my memoirs of the old days on working boats when he published the first article I sent to him. I am also grateful for permission to use some of the material published in subsequent editions of the magazine.

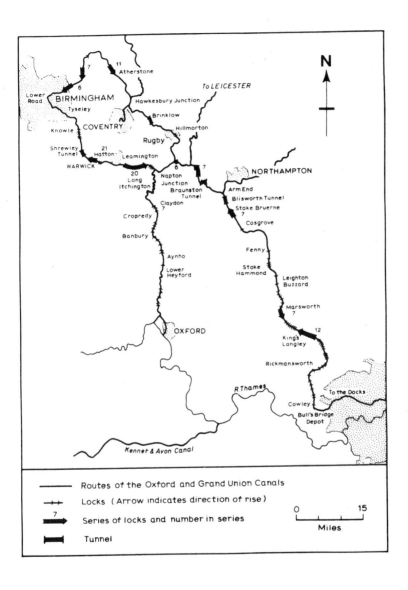

N

Lower Road

7 ── Atherstone

6 ── BIRMINGHAM

Tyseley

Hawkesbury Junction

COVENTRY

Brinklow

Hillmorton

Knowle

Rugby

Shrewley Tunnel

21 Hatton

Leamington

WARWICK

20 Long Itchington

6 Napton Junction

7

Braunston Tunnel

To LEICESTER

NORTHAMPTON

Arm End

Blisworth Tunnel

Stoke Bruerne

7

Claydon 7

Cropredy

Cosgrove

Banbury

Fenny

Aynho

Stoke Hammond

Lower Heyford

Leighton Buzzard

Marsworth 7

OXFORD

King's Langley 12

Rickmansworth

R Thames

To the Docks

Cowley

Bull's Bridge Depot

Kennet & Avon Canal

───── Routes of the Oxford and Grand Union Canals

→→→ Locks (Arrow indicates direction of rise)

7 Series of locks and number in series

Tunnel

0 ────── 15

Miles

The Grand Union and Oxford Canals

Author's Preface

The scheme for training women to work on canal boats was sponsored by the Inland Waterways department of the Ministry of Transport during the 1939–45 war, when pairs of boats were laid up for lack of crews. The scheme was proposed by Molly, who had worked her own boat, the Heather Bell, on the Sharpness canal, in discussion with Miss Minn and others at the Ministry. Finally, in 1942, the Grand Union Carrying Company based at Southall in Middlesex, decided to give the scheme a trial. Molly and Kit Gayford trained with the Sibleys, boatpeople who worked the boats Edgeware and Purley (see Eily Gayford's book *Amateur Boatwomen*), and they, in turn, trained the new recruits. Each trainer took three new trainees on a pair of boats for two round trips from the docks at Brentford or Limehouse to Birmingham, then round the Birmingham/Fazeley canal to the coalfields around Coventry and back down the Grand Union to deliver coal to factories alongside the canal. After two such arduous trips, lasting about six weeks, the trainees were considered capable of working on their own pairs of boats. When Molly left the boats, Daphne French became the second trainer, and it was with her that I trained.

Recruitment for women trainees was never as strongly promoted as recruitment for the Land Army or the three allied Services. Like many others who came – and went, I had seen only an insignificant advertisement in a women's magazine; but I knew at once that it was for me. I was interviewed by Miss Minn, given a medical examination and told to join Daphne on her boats Capricorn and Cleopatra at the Maida Vale stop. We were paid by the MOT a minimum wage of £2 a week during training and £3 a week when we qualified as crew. No uniform or extra clothing coupons were issued; Kit applied for the extra cheese ration allocated to land workers but the only response was a stock of

Lord Woolton's pies (for which he will ever be remembered!) to be bought from the shop at the top of Buckby locks.

We were a small band of women, probably only about thirty of us who stayed for any length of time, who grew to love the changing scenes on the canals and our way of life on the boats. Many, like myself, were drawn by romantic notions of travelling the canals, engendered by reading A. P. Herbert's *Water Gipsies*. For some the romance survived the arduous trials of reality so that we endured the rigours of weather, food-rationing and unaccustomed physical toil to achieve some of the confidence and expertise of the boatpeople themselves.

The scheme ended in 1946, when some of the boatmen returned to their families and at a time when the number of working boats was diminishing for lack of cargoes, lack of proper maintenance on boats and canals, and an upsurge of transportation by road eroding transport by water. The women trainees were left with no alternative but to return from whence they came.

Working on the boats was an incisive and memorable slice of experience, so that waterways and boats became an integral part of my life – and remain so, in spirit if not in actuality.

M.C.

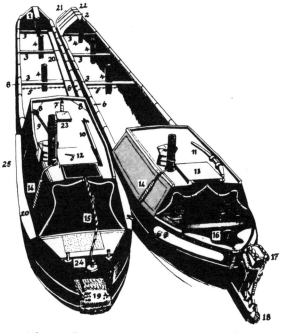

Motor Boat   Butty Boat

KEY TO BOATS

1. Cratch	14. Lamb's tail Fender
2. Mast	15. Swan's neck
3. Cross Beams	16. Stud and checking strap
4. Supports for Top planks	17. Turk's head
5. Chains for tightening	18. Fender
6. Rolled and Oiled Side cloths	19. Tipcats
7. Exhaust chimney	20. Gunwales
8. Oil tanks	21. Top strings
9. Mops	22. Tent-like structure
10. Short Shaft	23. Pigeon Box
11. Tiller	24. Dollies
12. Windlass	25. Sidedoors to Engine Room
13. Hatch cover	

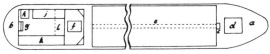

Length 70 feet   Beam 7 feet

KEY TO BOAT PLAN

(a). Fore-end	(g). Steps to Cabin
(b). Counter	(h). Kitchen range
(c). Headlight	(j). Lockers, Cupboards and Drawers
(d). Metal Hatch Cover	(k). Side bed
(e). Top planks	(l). 2nd bed
(f). Engine (18 h.p. Diesel)	

A canal pair: motor-boat and butty boat

1. *Nostalgia*

A lifetime ago, I thought, as I leaned against the rough stone coping of the bridge and looked down into the thick, shadowed water of the canal below me. A lifetime ago. Did we really travel this road up from Regent's Canal Dock northwards through Ricky, Casey, Berker, Maffas, Leighton, Fenney, Stoke, Armend, under the bridge where I was now standing and on up through Buckby and Braunston, Wigrams, Hatton, Knowle, Catty Barnes to Tyseley? The old names trickled through my mind as I scooped up the loose, crumbled mortar from the wall and let it trickle through my fingers to settle and sink into the smooth, unruffled surface darkened by the shadow of the bridge.

Those years ago. I saw again the pair of loaded boats, low down in the water and sheeted up against the weather, the motor distanced from the butty – its mate – by a seventy-foot length of snubber (towing line). Living and working on such a pair for almost two years had been an interlude in my life made possible by the need for women crews to replace the men who had been called up to fight the war – the war which had disrupted and destroyed so many plans and hopes and expectations.

I remembered the feelings of blind panic when the reality of war and its implications for me . . . ME . . . could no longer be ignored. It was like being sucked into a vortex where I no longer had control, or even an illusion of control, over the events which threatened to submerge me; where no future, either immediate or distant, was predictable and where I felt bombarded by the slogans and clichés which challenged, undermined and destroyed dearly held beliefs and convictions about my own attitudes to violence and war. I had felt betrayed, assaulted, violated, and there were times I envied the men who were being killed. Death seemed preferable to the chaos of living. But the obstinacy of survival fought back through the despair, the sense of blight, the panic.

The gloom of my nostalgic self-pity was broken by the welcome sound of a diesel engine slow-thumping its way southwards and I crossed to the other side of the bridge to see what would be coming. At the same time a burst of sound challenged my ears from the direction in which I had been gazing, the highly revved sound of a boat travelling at speed, and I turned away with irritation to watch the slower, predictable progress of the boat coming south. It was the Jaguar. Even from the distance of the bridge I knew the boat, recognized the old familiar shape of the cratch, the glimpse of white plastic bags of coal neatly stacked in the hold and the slouched figure at the tiller. I knew that it was taking coal from a small pit by the Ashby canal to the top of Stoke locks, where it was stored for a local delivery service – an effort to keep the old ways alive.

I was aware of the sporadic attempts to renew the commercial usage for which the canals were built – a grain run from Blisworth to Manchester, barrels of oil from Chester to Birmingham and coal southwards from the almost derelict coalfields. Sadly I reflected that there was never a hope of any permanent renewal of trade. The young enthusiasts really had their roots elsewhere, and the difficulties of maintaining a steady flow of delivery for even one canalside factory soon defeated their romantic intentions. I thought of the factories where we had delivered forty to forty-five tons of coal every three weeks or so – Heinz, Nestlé's, Glaxo, ABC, Croxley and Langley papermills, all built alongside the canal. There was always a steady string of boats waiting to offload, a continuously moving conveyor-belt of supplies, with coal from the pits around Coventry and imported goods northwards from the docks at Brentford and Commercial Road. The supply of coal to the factories had to be constant and predictable in order to be a viable enterprise and, at present, these lone Walter Mittys had no hope, however purposeful and well-intentioned their efforts.

I became aware that the boat speeding north would likely meet the Jaguar in the narrowness of the bridge'ole, or near enough for discomfort. The steerer would not hear the Jaguar's engine above the roar of its own, and the Jaguar was unlikely to throttle back sufficiently to allow the other boat to take precedence through the bridge. Steerers on the few working boats still asserted that they had right of way over the pleasure craft, and the threat of a possible ramming by those implacable bows of a seventy-footer weighted with twenty tons of cargo ensured that this right was maintained. My accustomed ears registered that the steerer on the Jaguar had throttled down in order to negotiate his length of boat around the bend which led through to the bridge'ole.

For a second I maliciously anticipated the imminent crash. The shock might teach the steerer of the speeding cruiser a much-needed lesson so that in future he'd approach bridge'oles, especially the 'blind' ones, with the caution and care needed for a safe passage. The moment passed and I rushed to his side of the bridge waving my arms in the time-old manner to warn him of the approaching Jaguar. There was a slight change in the engine's revs – not enough, not enough. The impact was inevitable and I closed my eyes as the Jaguar nosed through the narrow space below. Shouts of fear and rage tore upwards from the cruiser as it swerved into the muddy shallows to avoid the menacing bows of the heavy coalboat. Lost his nerve, I thought, keeping well back from view. The Jaguar slid through, unperturbed by the shouts and threats, the steerer slouched behind the protection of the chimney with his back towards the unfortunate cruiser, which was slewing round helplessly in the wash, its bows firmly embedded in the pile-up of mud by the bridge. I had retreated to the shelter of some blackthorn bushes at the end of the bridge where I could watch without being seen. Heads bristled from each end of the cruiser while the Jaguar continued on its way without a backward glance from Andy, who was steering. The steerer of the cruiser, resplendent in Aran pullover and yachting cap, was shouting instructions and counter-instructions to his crew. I felt like offering advice but refrained. I knew from experience how my interference would be regarded by the man in his own self-appointed area of male superiority. They'd get off eventually, if no other boats were passing.

But there were always other boats these days and, down the Cut, in the wake of the Jaguar, came a flotilla of inflatables powered by outboard engines. I counted four of them and decided not to wait. Such scenes as inevitably must follow had long since ceased to amuse me. My sympathies and allegiance were all with the Jaguar and other loners in their efforts to link the present with a fractured past, and once again I felt a violent rush of antagonism to all these other usurpers. My reason reluctantly admitted the inevitability of the present scene, with the fleets of hire-boats, the marinas, the gift shops, the swarms of tourists and gongoozlers – a term used by boatpeople for curious onlookers – the jumbled agglomeration of craft with which the waterways were now infested. How long would the present invasion last? I hoped it would pass before the canals were reduced to a state of hopeless disrepair. Locusts, I thought vehemently, locusts, and turned my back on the ensuing chaos of craft and crews about to erupt in the canal below me.

I wondered, not for the first time, at the glib advertisements on the glossy brochures which state that anyone can take a boat on the canals with absolute safety. How long was it before we were let loose with a boat? I remembered the six arduous weeks of training – two round trips – and even then we were only allowed to go as crew with the more experienced steerers who had charge of a pair. It took months of living and working on the boats before those of us who stayed the course began to enjoy the competence and expertise practised and perfected by generations of the boatpeople themselves.

I walked slowly back along a lane, then a road, across another bridge and back on to the towpath to the small wharf where my own boat (*see* Pl. 16) was tied. I had walked out to rid myself of yet another irritation. I had been in the engine-room checking the oil and giving the engine a much-needed clean and polish. The fresh feel of spring never fails to spur me into tackling jobs which I have been quite content to ignore through the cold winter months. The boat had given a sudden lurch . . . then another . . . and another. I emerged to see a total stranger disappearing into the well-deck and the movement of others in the saloon. I shouted at the retreating back but she turned and smiled sweetly, saying that the man in the shop said they could take a 'peek'. The 'man' could only have been another visitor, as Irene was in charge that day. I fumed on the bank and shouted at them to get off while they continued their tour through the boat, commenting on the lace plates and the copper pipes. No doubt I should have been flattered at their appreciation of my beautiful boat, but to me they were brash and impertinent boors, insensitive to the paramount law of the Cut in which I had been trained, that of respect for the privacy of others. To make my point after they had left, I went up to their splendid motor caravan and stared in through the open doorway.

'Come in and have a coffee,' said one of the young women. 'Sorry about your boat. We guessed it was on show.'

'Another time,' I replied, my churlish rancour disarmed by her show of friendliness.

Why did *I* have to feel guilty about my hostility to their interest? I had returned to the engine-room and masochistically decided that a change of oil was necessary!

I recalled the incident somewhat ruefully as I made my way back to the yard and to the boat which had been our home for the past five years.

Why did I feel increasingly so resentful and hostile to the interest, often warm and genuine, shown to my boat by the casual visitors to the yard and by the week-enders on their own boats who come out from the towns and cities to take a trip from the marina, relax and enjoy a chat over a pint at the local. Even the word 'marina' makes me shudder as I use it reluctantly; such an alien concept to my own feelings for the canals – like pinning a cheap piece of jewellery on a tailored tweed suit. I edged around a water-filled gap in the towpath. Part of my trouble was that I was trying to compromise between the demands of two vastly differ-ent life-styles; perhaps it would be easier when I retired in a few months time. Or would it? I would always feel an alien in the present tarted-up image of the canals. My love for the waterways and the nomadic way of life was rooted in the more realistic, purposeful and meaningful usage for which the canals initially had been built. My early experiences of living and working on the boats for the Grand Union Canal Carrying Company had shaped my feelings and attitudes to the waterways so that the present scene would always seem tawdry, anachronistic, capricious and

transient, as if the 'road', as we called the canal, was being prosti-
tuted and exploited by the vast numbers of entrepreneurs who had
recognized an opportunity to 'make a fast buck', as they say. Not
entirely true either; many of them are quite as dedicated as myself.
The success of their enterprises depends upon the continued
viability of the canal system. The possibility of profit always
provides an incentive and, with luck, the caring motive eventually
can supersede the purely mercenary.

I saw the Jaguar just ahead, and Andy's lurcher dog emerged
from a gap in the hedge. We looked at each other for a second or
two, and then he was off to rejoin his boat in the bridge'ole before
the yard. I perched myself on an overgrown stile to see what else
would be passing and to eat the apple I had brought with me. I
wanted those inflatables out of the way before I returned to the
Alphons.

In my mind's eye I saw again a pair of working boats sheeted up
and low down in the water, a boat's length of towing line between
them. Why had I ever left the boats, I wondered, not for the first
time. But, forty years ago, *we* had been the outsiders, newcomers
and alien to the lives and ways of the boatpeople themselves.
They always referred to us as 'the trainees', however long we had
worked alongside them, however expert we gradually became
and however much we adapted our ways to their own. We all
left the boats when the hostilities of defence and vengeance
dwindled into a no-man's land of uncertainty, into a hiatus
between the frenzy of war and the frenetic activities powered
by ambitions and greed which were soon to germinate in that
narcotic vacuum.

After the war there was a period of halcyon years for the
amateur lover of waterways when the commercial traffic had
almost ceased and before the hire companies began to proliferate.
Gradually, from the lull and the quietude had germinated the
furore of the present scene, with the fleets of smartly painted
boats, their crews of naked bodies strewn along the cabin tops and
the locksides; with the plushy canalside pubs where occasionally
I join friends and listen to the in-talk and chatter about personalities, prize-winning marathons of travelling, the relative merits
and de-merits of engines, hulls, hire companies, boatbuilders,
insurance-brokers, mooring prices, marinas, shops, souvenirs. I
think of old Sid and others like him who have lived long enough

to relish, albeit somewhat cynically, the bonanza of popularity which has overtaken them and their old associations with the canals so that they have become 'characters' to be treated to as many pints as they can hold – and more! – by the avid collectors of authenticity.

There are times when I feel like a museum piece myself! My own boat, the Alphons, is a compromise between a functional past and the present glamorized scene. It had been a working butty, had been lovingly restored by a dedicated boatbuilder, and a cabin built over the length of the hold, the long, slim lines, the traditional colours and graining faithfully reproduced in my ark-like home.

There was no sight or sound of the inflatables. A soft, light rain was beginning to brush the long grass at my feet and the tangle of thorn sprays with a fine, silvery mist. No doubt they and the hire-boat had returned to the comforts of the pub near the marina. Piously I hoped there had been no serious damage to crews or craft back at the bridge.

As I clambered down from my perch, other, less glamorized scenes from the present bonanza of holidays afloat came to mind. There are days when the rain falls solidly and persistently, turning the towpath and boatyard into a muddy quagmire, when tired and sullen-looking wives transport the remnants of a wearisome holiday back to the comforts of their waiting cars while their disgruntled and aggressive husbands seek to offload their frustrations, disillusions and resentment in a stream of complaints directed at the hire-boat operator or anyone else who might be around.

Incidents and even tragedies thread through many of these casual and carefree holidays on the Cut; there are so many hazards ready to ambush the over-confident and the foolhardy. Even the experts in the old days had not been immune. There was that baby tied too loosely to the chimney so that it had broken loose and fallen over the side in a lock; its head had been crushed between the boat and the lockside before it was rescued. And the young boy who slipped on the icy concrete, fell in and was drowned; never came up, they said. All the trainees had heard of the loaded boat which had struck the concrete coping in the bridge'ole at the top of Atherstone so that the boat was swamped and sank within seconds. There were fingers mutilated by ropes, bones broken and bruised from faulty winding gear on the lock gates. I remember how the catch of such a paddle on one of the Stone locks in recent years had slipped so that the windlass had flown off to deal my son a frightening blow at the side of his face. Most lessons were learned through hard, punishing experience and there are few who escape without some painful reminder of their trips along the waterways. My own twinges still remind me of past mishaps on the boats.

More recently we had all been shocked at the news of a tragedy at Cromwell weir on the Trent: three, or was it five, drowned? Canals would always claim their victims.

The yard was quiet, with no one around as I undid the cratch cover and climbed into the well-deck and into the warmth of the saloon. The fire glowed red through the mica panels of the stove doors, and the copper pipes which led to the three radiators down the boat were pleasantly warm to the chill of my hands. I hung up my anorak to dry in the small yet functional bathroom. I sat on the settee-couch to enjoy the warmth and comfort of the fire as I sipped my mug of hot tea. Through the window opposite I could see a heron standing on the bank, immobile yet poised for instant take-off at the slightest hint of sound which posed a threat for the vulnerability of his stance. The herons, the swans, the moorhens, the mallards and even the water rats – all had learned the necessity of discretion and flight at the approach of voices and the noisy petrol-driven engines. The otters which, in the old days, we occasionally glimpsed in the reeds above Aynho, had disappeared long since. There were sorry tales of 'cowboys' who rammed and scattered any groups of birds with the boats they hired or brought on trailers for a day's 'excitement' on the canal. However, today had been relatively quiet – the rain was often such a blessing!

I prolonged the precious minutes of tea and leisure. The red-gold gleam of the parana pine panelling glowed in the soft light from the fire. Simmy, the cat, was bunched on the top of the piano, his favourite perch from where he was able to watch the small, busy movements in the bank opposite. I would soon have to move; there were lecture notes to be checked and revised and notes to be made for a talk I was to give later in the week to a group of waterways enthusiasts in Peterborough.

It was dark and the cabin lights were dimming. I'd have to run

the engine for a couple of hours to recharge the batteries. Reluctantly I emerged. The boat lay snugly against the side, and I
lowered an old car tyre from the cabin roof on its length of line in
case a wind should blow up in the night. The rain had drifted on
its way westwards, and stars were beginning to prick their
designs in the darkening sky. I clambered down into the cold,
metallic smell of the engine-room, pushed the ignition button
and stood there to check on the shafting and the alternator as the
whole solid bulk of engine warmed into a slow, easy rhythm. I
checked that the shaft was not turning and then slightly moved
the accelerator cable to increase the revs. I thought of the old
routine on the Hercules and the Hyperion, boats on which I had
been the steerer. It had been my responsibility to crawl into the
engine-room before the other two were awake, and to prime
the engine with an implement called a pricker. The object of the
operation had been explained to me many times but without any
lasting understanding on my part; it was a mechanical operation
which produced the desired effect; if I did it, the engine was likely
to fire at the first or second effort to swing the great flywheel.
With trousers and pullover pulled hastily over pyjamas, I would
crawl round the gunwale to perform the ritual of the prime, and
then I'd shout at the still-sleeping crew that it was up-time.

I took a last look round the engine-room to make sure that all
was in order and returned to the comfort of the saloon and felt
glad, with the lethargy of age, that the daily chores of fighting
with the engine, shifting batteries, shifting cargoes to keep the
boats on an even level and scrubbing out the holds to remove the
last elusive grains of wheat or barley to spare ourselves later
smells from rotting corn, remained only as memories. They no
longer existed as necessary chores to sap my energy and the thin
reserves of my equanimity.

I shovelled more phurnacite into the stove, poured myself a
sherry and wondered why it was the hard, difficult part of the
work which came most readily to mind. There had been plenty of
good days when the boats went well, when there were no
mishaps and when a visit to the pub had seemed the perfect
ending to a perfect day. Perhaps, like the news bulletins, it was
the bad news which made the headlines most of the time.
However, those early mornings I'd never forget and I shivered at
the memory of them as I looked with even greater appreciation at

the comforts of the Alphons. There was no need to travel or to remain tied up at base except to please my mood of the moment; and, almost immediately, I began to plan a trip for the Easter holiday, when Helen would be at home to join me. We might brave the continuous locking down to London, tie up for a few days in Little Venice to visit friends and go to a theatre. Or we might make another trip down the Oxford at a time of the year when the shallow pounds, replenished with spring rains, would still be navigable before the summer droughts. I looked at the maps and guidebooks as I ate the remains of a cottage pie and decided that we would go southwards. Possibly an unsuspecting friend of Helen's would join us for a 'holiday' to help with the locking!

Meanwhile there were the notes to be made about working on the canal boats during the war. I took out my old journal to check that the markers were still in place for the passages I would read. Diaries and journals provide such popular and widespread sources for biographies, autobiographies and research programmes on the famous against their backdrop of large political and social events; and also on the less famous with their specialized interests and insights into the small intimacies of their daily lives. My own diaries, written sporadically over the years in an untidy sprawl, fill several exercise books. Most of them contain outpourings from the neurotic confusions of a youth long past, but in this volume I had recorded the more practical daily events of an experience which is almost obsolete and has become the subject of nostalgic reminiscence to be revived in story and dramatic re-enactment.

One day, perhaps, I'd encapsulate my own memories and records into a book. And then I thought ruefully of all the shelves of autobiographies of those who are household names. We have become such a nation of literates despite all the gloomy prognostications of the educational pessimists! My thoughts ran on as I thumbed through the well-worn pages and arranged a few slides to punctuate the talk. Luckily there were always plenty of questions to enliven the monotony of a lecture into the dynamics of dialogue and discussion.

I picked up the small logbook we had tried to keep written up on the Hercules and Cetus boats, and my eye caught a fairly typical entry: '1 June [1945]. *Continuous engine trouble. Blocked fuel pipe.'* If only we had had that beautiful Lister HR2 instead.of that water-cooled, broken-down old National, how much easier our lives would have been!

As I continued to sit, with the steady and predictable thump of the engine from the back end of the boat softly affirming the silence, an image from the past flicked into my retrospections. Three female figures, untalking, unwashed, unfed, took up their stations in the restricted space of the engine-room. The great flywheel threatened their puny efforts with its massive immobility. The two strongest gripped the length of the starting-handle while the third stood tensed to push over the compression lever at the critical moment of possible ignition. It was still dark – or that is how my memory reflected the image – as we always reckoned to be off before first light. No word was spoken as the two slowly turned the handle to swing the flywheel into action. Momentum was speeded by a maximum effort from the two bending shapes. 'One – two – three – NOW,' shouted one, and the suspense as the compression lever was pushed over ended in either a dull, depressed thud or in a hopeful cough and a tentative chug. 'Accelerator – QUICK,' but already a hand had pulled on the speed cable, and the flywheel would turn with growing confidence. The brass pumps launched into their own alternate rhythms, and a thin trickle of water from the cooling outlet was watched hopefully by one of the team as she leaned outside. 'Working?' asked another tensely. 'Batteries?' asked the third. They all knew what each other meant without further explanation. The needle indicated a charge and they knew that there would be power enough for the headlights and the small bulb in each cabin.

I shivered at the memory of those early mornings on the working boats and reluctantly levered myself from the saloon of the Alphons to turn off the engine. I switched off the fuel intake and took a final look around with an even greater appreciation of the modernized version of the engine-room. I returned to a last mug of cocoa and a read before bed. I slept fitfully, the random images and garbled recordings from the past flickering and consolidating into half-remembered scenes and events, with myself as participator and onlooker at the same time. I awoke early, still tired. One day I would have to exorcize the memories by externalizing them into the form of a book. One day, when I retire, I temporized. Everyone told me I'd need a project when the time came.

The day arrived, somewhat more rapidly than I anticipated. After the first euphoric phase of an intoxicating sense of freedom, during which I travelled on the Alphons to London, Leicester, Manchester, Oxford and on through the network of canals, the predicted reaction finally overtook me. I needed something more to bridge the gap between a working life and a life of continued leisure. I needed a purpose to consume and direct the still recurrent creative impulses. No longer was there any excuse to delay what had to be done – to get that book written.

I took the Alphons to a secluded mooring, with only the moorhens and an occasional heron for company, and began to write . . .

2. A Step Sideways

'How and why did you become a bargee?' is the common question asked by the curious.

The answer isn't as simple and direct as the questioner supposes. There are many factors related to temperament, previous experience and force of circumstance which determine individual action and which so often culminate in what appears to be an impulsive and unconsidered decision. Looking back, I wonder if I could have done otherwise.

Often, when asked, I give the romantic and direct reply which is half expected: I stood on a bridge over Regent's Park Canal and watched two barges thread their way down the narrow strip of water into the heart of London and decided that, one day, I too would stand at the tiller of such a barge and go travelling through city and countryside. Unfortunately, like so many others, I had never noticed the canals, had never lived near one and, like my questioners, referred to all traffic on them as 'barges'. It is only since I worked on the boats (note that narrow boats—boats of seven foot beam—should be called 'boats' not 'barges') that I lean over bridges and walk along towpaths and, when in London, make my pilgrimage to Maida Vale, Camden, Old Ford and even Commercial Road to feel, in retrospect, the thrill of standing at the tiller of a narrowboat as it threads its way into the heart of the city.

'Force of circumstance' is another over-simplified reply to the more persistent questioners. 'I received a telegram on 12 July 1944 from the local Education Authority (London) stating that I should evacuate immediately with groups of unknown children to an unknown destination – or resign.' Obviously I resigned. Those who knew me smile equivocally.

'But why a bargee?' they persist.

'I don't really know,' I reply more or less honestly, so that casual curiosity usually is satisfied.

In fact, the decision to join the boats was made almost incidentally.

'What on earth will you do?' asked friends in Student Movement House where I had been declaiming against the inflexibility of bureaucratic procedures.

'I'll become a bargee,' I said in a moment of bravado.

One of my friends took me seriously and brought me an old magazine with a Letters-to-the-Editor section in which the question, 'How do I become a bargee?' was answered with an address of the wartime MOT Inland Waterways Department. I could do no less than write and, rather to my surprise, I had an immediate reply from a Miss Minn, whose sister was suffering from the same peremptory treatment by the LEA as myself.

'Any previous experience of boats?' she asked. I told her of my sailing holidays on the Broads. 'You can forget all that,' she replied briefly. 'Work on the boats is totally different, and your knowledge of sail will be of no use whatever.'

'Can you swim?' was her next question. I assured her that I was a good swimmer.

'Why didn't you join one of the Services?' She was a persistent interviewer, and some inner voice counselled caution.

'Teaching is a reserved occupation,' I replied lamely, 'and until I received the telegram I had no thought of doing anything else.'

She seemed satisfied.

I had learned to be reticent about my strongly held convictions as a pacifist. I remember how horrified I had been when friends I had admired rushed off in the early months of the 1939 war to don the blue and khaki uniforms of the armed forces. All our serious idealisms and discussions dissolved into nebulous fancies as they responded to the urgency of patriotic fervour. I had taken our idealisms seriously and was left on the touchline as they joined in the great surges towards a goal called victory.

Also I concealed the fact that my teaching career had been anything but consistent and 'dedicated'. When the onset of war negated a scholarship to study at the Sorbonne, I packed a rucksack and went off to Oxford, where I became one of the first 'clippies' – a bus-conductress. How I enjoyed the freedom and movement of the red buses as we picked up and disgorged through the busy streets of the city. I lived in a gipsy caravan – gaily painted like the boats and found a pitch close by the river and Iffley lock. The lock held no particular interest for me except as a slightly menacing place after dark. I only remember walking along the canal towpath on a dreary, wet day and not being very impressed by its muddy route through the north end of the city – not worth a second visit. Then events converged to end my work with the Oxford Bus Company, and I took a flat in London with a friend whose pilot husband had recently been killed. I returned to teaching in a Central school.

It didn't seem necessary to disclose the vagaries of those uncertain years. I was one of the teachers who had received the infamous telegram, and Miss Minn's sister had been another; she understood my gesture of resignation. Despite her disparaging reference to my sailing experience, I was 'in'.

'I'll put you with Daphne French,' she said. 'She's one of the two trainers. I'm sure you'll like her. Her boats are the Capricorn and the Cleopatra, and you can join them at the Maida Vale stop. Take as few belongings as possible – there isn't much room . . . and you'll need a strong leather belt.'

Once again I packed my well-worn rucksack. I knew how to condense my needs to its confines – and my home-made sleeping-bag was still serviceable.

The Capricorn and the Cleopatra were there. Until I actually saw the two slim, unfamiliar shapes with their empty, business-like holds and with the letters GUCCC (Grand Union Canal Carrying Company) in bold blue paint mathematically spaced out on the sides of the cabins, I don't think I believed in the reality of the decision I'd taken to become a 'bargee'. I don't think I believed that such a way of life existed outside the pages of A. P. Herbert's *Water Gipsies*, let alone that I was now about to become one of those almost mythical characters. I stood there looking at the boats, uncertain of the appropriate announcement that I had arrived.

'Hallo,' I called apprehensively and was relieved to elicit an immediate response. A fresh-faced woman with brown hair and spectacles looked out of the square opening at the cabin end of the boat nearest to me.

'You must be Margaret,' she said in a soft, pleasant voice; hadn't Miss Minn said that she was Irish?

'Come aboard,' she said as I unhitched my rucksack. 'Good, not too much luggage, I see.' She took my bedroll while I put a long leg over the side of the small well-deck and then peered down into the cabin I would share with this unknown person for the next weeks.

I was soon to appreciate that this cabin was luxury compared with the cabin on the motor occupied by two other learners. I looked across at the narrow, workmanlike deck (the counter) of the other boat, considering the few inches of freeboard between the sturdy yet diminutive deck and the dark, dirty water of the canal.

'Come on down,' called Daphne from the dark interior. 'Backwards,' she added. 'It's easier. The other two have gone off to shop. We'll have a pot of tea and I'll show you round. I hope they won't be long. I'd like to make the docks this evening.'

I turned around and carefully lowered my length down through the hatchway. There was a convenient step halfway down the drop to the floor of the cabin – the lid of the coal box, as I soon discovered.

'If you sit on the step for the moment, I'll just explain where everything is,' said Daphne. 'Then you can unpack while I make the tea.'

Obediently I turned to survey the interior of the home I was to share with this stranger who smiled at me reassuringly. I needed no such reassurance: the cabin reminded me at once of my home in the gipsy caravan at Iffley. The same fierce little fire was burning in the shiny black-leaded range to my left, sending its warmth through the cabin and almost burning my leg through the protection of my well-worn skiing trousers.

'It gets too hot in here most of the time so we have to keep the doors open,' said Daphne as she lowered a gaily painted panel to reveal a cupboard with shelves of crockery and tins.

'The larder,' she explained measuring the precious tea into a red enamel teapot. 'Have you brought your emergency ration cards?' I assured her that I had.

'Not much more to show you,' she said and lowered a larger flap just beyond the 'larder' so that the flap rested on a ledge of the two-foot-wide bench which took up the whole length of the cabin side on my right.

'Two beds,' she continued in her soft, distinctive voice. 'One along and one across. We fold the beds up into the cupboard during the day.'

There was a smaller cupboard up over, two large and capacious drawers underneath – one at each side – locker space under the top panels of the side bench and another small cupboard to my right with space underneath for a person's head – or feet! Cosy living indeed for two! However, it was all so familiar that I felt at home immediately. Rooms and houses cluttered with furniture and belongings have never held much appeal for me; the care of them takes up so much valuable time and energy.

'Where would you like to sleep?' asked Daphne. 'Across or along?' I wasn't sure of the implications.

She suggested that I should sleep in the cupboard as she slept along the side-bed to make the early morning tea. She said that she could reach everything without getting out of bed – an arrangement more fully appreciated when the weather grew colder! My head would go in the cupboard and hers would go under the cupboard to my right so that our feet would meet in the corner!

'You're tall,' she said, 'but I think we shall manage. The boatpeople are mostly small, and that double bed [Three feet six wide!] has to take two of them; a child or two on the side-bed and spare babies in the big drawers where we keep our clothes.'

I began to appreciate that there were only two of us to share this compacted living space and, as the days passed, I also grew to appreciate that it was Daphne with whom I was to share the intimacies of living and working in those narrow confines. Ten years older than myself, she was the most tolerant and kindly person who accepted my moods and my irrational and unpredictable behaviour without a reproach.

As we drank the scalding tea from the thick utility-type mugs, Daphne explained that we were off to Regent's Canal dock to load up with billets of steel for Tyseley, then we would take the Lower Road through the back streets of Birmingham to load up with coal from one of the coalfields around Coventry to supply one of the canalside factories on our way back down the Grand Union. She explained that a round trip would take about three weeks. An experienced crew would do it in half the time but on the training boats we would work a nine-to-five day with a tie-up for lunch – depending upon weather and conditions. There were gauging-points along the route to check on cargoes and the movement of the boats.

'What happens if you break down or there's an accident?' I asked.

'You have to look for a phone-box to report back. Not too easy along some stretches unless you happen to know there's a village somewhere around. I suppose you haven't a map?' she asked. 'It would be such a help. Usually it's quicker and easier to send a message by passing boats,' she added as I shook my head in reply to her query.

Her capable hands were already rinsing her mug in a few inches of water tipped from a large covered can painted red. 'Have to be careful with water.' She explained that we filled up the cans at the few water points along the route. There were just two cans for each boat – one was kept inside and one on the roof. I knew all about the value of water on board a boat – there was a firm custom aboard the Return (the sailing boat owned by my friends) that everyone licked the plates clean to make washing up a mere formality.

I rinsed my own mug and then dragged in my rucksack and bedroll. My bed consisted of a thin flock palliasse, two grey army blankets interlapped to form a bag and a thin cotton sleeping-bag inside again for the lining. I had slept in this home-made bag in haystacks, on beds of heather and bracken, on beaches and in barns, and it had proved its resistance to night winds and even frosts. Large safety pins kept the blankets in place, and in those days I slept through my eight hours without even ruffling the cotton lining. There were times on the Cleopatra when we slept in socks and pullovers to pad further our home-made cocoons. A strip of foam rubber and a warmly padded and zipped sleeping-bag would have added a touch of real luxury to our spartan existence!

Daphne left me to unpack while she went round to prime the engine. She hoped the other two wouldn't be long. It was time to be off. The words sounded like music to me – time to be off, time to be off.

Hastily I stowed my bedroll in the cupboard, my clothes and few possessions in the capacious drawer and my rucksack in the locker space under the side-bed along with an assortment of footwear, an axe, a flue-brush, a large hammer and a sizeable box of tinned evaporated milk. I was just about to peer into the contents of the small cupboard by the door when I heard voices on the bank. I was curious to see who would be my fellow trainees for the next six weeks – or the two round trips considered necessary to prove the worth, or otherwise, of aspiring 'bargees'. As I peered out, a large netted bag of vegetables and another of packages were dumped on to the deck in front of me. Behind the bags a pair of solid-looking feet encased in shapeless canvas shoes appeared and, as I looked upwards, I remember thinking that this woman was hardly the agile type I associated with boatwork. She was about my own height but very solid looking – like her feet! She was followed by the fourth member of this oddly assorted crew, slim and dark, good-looking, nervous. Daphne had reappeared and there were brief introductions – Bash, Mary, Margaret.

Bash – what a name! – lurched over to the motor cabin with the bags. Mary smiled nervously and said that they had joined only the day before – at Bull's Bridge. Lord, I thought, those two in a cabin even smaller than this. She seemed fragile, well educated and as unsuitable in her way as Bash was in hers.

'Ready?' called Daphne as she perched in the entrance to the engine-room. Bash grumbled that she was hungry – she was always hungry, and I sympathized! I poured two mugs of well-watered tea for the newcomers as Daphne continued with her instructions. We would go breasted up – meaning that the boats would proceed tied together at stern and bows – as far as Islington tunnel, where the boats would then be singled out. Mary and I were detailed to help start the engine.

Mary moved delicately along the gunwale between the boats and I followed. There was hardly room for the three of us as the great hunk of green painted metal girded with unfamiliar levers, brass rods, caps and cylinders filled most of the space. A large flywheel was suspended immobile above an opening in the metal floorboards below which I caught a glimpse of black, oily fluid – the bilges, I thought.

'Mary, you pull over the compression lever at "three". Margaret, you hold the starting handle with me – not like that. You could break a thumb if it backfires.' I was beginning to feel as nervous as Mary's clenched face looked.

'Slowly at first – take the speed from me,' added Daphne. Slowly the flywheel began to revolve as the two of us turned the handle, and gradually the speed was increased until Daphne shouted, 'One, two, THREE.' Mary's moment of action had come; she pushed over a lever and the engine broke into a steady throb while Daphne gave it an extra burst by pulling on the acceleration cable – the governor rod, as I learned to call it.

The 'governor' was fixed to control the maximum speed at which the boats were allowed to travel. Some of the boatmen, especially those on the fly-boats (those who lived up to their names by travelling throughout the twenty-four hours, sometimes with a crew working on a rota system but often with the boatman and his mate snatching drifts of sleep whenever possible) tampered with the governor rods in order to increase the speed of their engines but they risked heavy penalties and possible dismissal if the adjustment was discovered. Undue speed, then as now, was the greatest menace to the proper maintenance of the canals and, as dredging and piling had to be kept to a minimum, it was in the Company's – and the boatpeople's – best interests to exercise the necessary control over the 'cowboys' whose record-beating marathons were regarded with suspicion rather than approval. Regular checks were made along the route when the trip card had to be produced and the depth of the boats gauged to ensure that the cargo had not been pilfered – so that the few, the very few, 'cowboys' were soon detected.

We all scrambled out of the engine-room. Bash was sitting on the deck side of Cleopatra drinking her tea and holding the remnant of an eccles cake.

'Can you untie, Margaret?' asked Daphne as she fitted a long brass tiller onto the curved helm, known as the swan's neck. The tiller was always removed when not in use as the heavy brass length could give a vicious swipe to anyone within its orbit and could wedge the boats against the wall of a lock when the rush of water against the rudder would make it swing wildly. The large curved wooden tiller of the butty was slotted upside down in a curved arc reaching upwards, like an overlarge sickle, into a groove in the wooden 'ellum' which was all of a piece with the massive wooden rudder. The 'ellum' of the butty was also known as the 'Turk's head' as it was usually decorated with plaitings of ropework and often with a horse's tail, a memento of past days.

'Pull out the butty tiller and put it along the cabin top.' The instructions followed clearly and firmly: 'You'll need a windlass for the Hampstead locks. Tuck it into your belt at the back. And DON'T LOSE IT. They're almost impossible to replace if you drop it overboard.' Guns and munitions were far more necessary than windlasses in those war-weary years.

The windlass (the 'iron' or the 'key' as it was often called) was the boatman's most prized possession. The implement was cast in a single mould and came from the foundry rough and hard to the hands. Most of the boatmen filed down the rougher ridges, and many fitted the handle with a cylinder of brass inside which the iron handle could turn without the usual wear and tear on the hands. The 'iron' was often the prized possession of a child, given as a birthday or Christmas present as soon as he was big enough to turn the winding gear on some of the easier locks. Sometimes the name of its owner was scratched or engraved into the metal, and often the metal was painted white so that it would be seen easily if left forgetfully by a lockside. A windlass was a personal possession and, even within the family, each windlass belonged exclusively to its owner. Like a favourite cricket bat, it had the right feel, handgrip, weight, balance which made it special for the owner. Possession was assured by the constant wearing of the windlass, either tucked into a leather belt in the crook of a back or slouched over a shoulder under the jacket so that the hump of it added a grotesque shape to the boatman's shoulders already bent with years of hauling and loading. So, it was always ready, at hand to wind the paddles, to be swung round in aggression, to be used as a hammer, scoop or any other makeshift device required for the variety of incidents which beset a boatman's existence.

The boatman had to pay for a lost iron, a further insurance to keep it jealously guarded. To lose it by dropping it into a depth of water or to leave it lying forgotten by a lockside was treated as a

crime even by the trainees. Lock-keepers had eyes for such abandoned treasures; if a pound was dredged or a lock emptied for
repairs, the salvage of lost irons provided a remunerative ad-
dition to his small wage. He would sell the spares for less than it
cost to buy a new one, and boatpeople would be only too glad to
take advantage of the cheaper price. But the lock-keepers
guarded their finds carefully and only as a special favour would
they be persuaded to part with a retrieved windlass.

Many of the women trainees, at first, were often clumsy,
careless and forgetful, and windlasses were frequently mislaid or
dropped into the water. But we learned quickly. 'Lend me your
windlass, mine's gone,' would be met with a stony response from
a more experienced trainee who had already learned that the
windlass was her most prized possession. You didn't lend your
windlass and you certainly were not expected to borrow. We
developed eyes which scoured the locksides in the hope that
another careless trainee had left a precious iron behind, and there
would seldom be any compunction about acquiring it even if the
owner was probably one of the crew on boats ahead. Without the
tool you stood around helplessly while the others over-
emphasized the extra work inflicted upon them by your careless-
ness. The only hope of finding a replacement was to persuade,
bribe, wheedle or flatter one of the more sympathetic lock-
keepers to part with one of his treasures.

'Your windlass. DON'T LOSE IT,' Daphne repeated as she
handed me the rough piece of iron from its safe storage in the
locker under her bed.

The instructions fluttered around in my head like birds. I
removed the arm of the butty tiller and carefully placed it along
the inside ridge of the cabin roof. There wasn't much space as the
hatch cover was pushed back and alongside was a mop with a
home-made rag head, a quant pole with a metal hooked end
which I soon learned to call the short shaft, a large water can and a
coil of rope.

'Can you untie, Margaret?' asked Daphne again. She looked at
Bash but decided to leave her to finish her tea. Mary was below in
the motor cabin. 'Front end first. Just coil the rope and leave it on
the for'ard deck. Then nip back, untie the stern rope and hop
aboard. All right?'

I nodded and was out on the bank before she had finished

talking, eager to prove my efficiency. I slipped the rope from the iron ring let into a slab of concrete on the towpath, and immediately the bows swung outwards before I could even begin to coil the length of rope. I halted the swing by pulling hard but the stern was too tightly tied to allow the bows any response to my efforts, and the length of rope slowly slipped through my hands.

'Throw it over the cratch,' shouted Daphne. 'Back here quick as you can.' I threw the rope hard across to the receding bows but it missed and the end was left trailing in the water. So much for my show of efficiency! I raced back to untie the stern while Bash continued to sit and drink her tea – her third? The first spurt of irritation at her passivity sent a small charge of resentment through me, no doubt quickened by my own show of incompetence. I untied the stern rope and threw the end across to her while I clambered aboard.

'Plenty of time,' said Daphne calmly. 'Just push the boats off from the side. Use the mop. Bash, finish your tea and then go up for'ard to coil the rope.'

Without looking at me, Bash left her mug on the floor of the deck and made her way along the narrow gunwale, then along the planks laid along the length of the empty hold, scrambled around the cratch at the for'ard end of the butty and gained the small front deck, where she slowly and laboriously retrieved the dripping length of rope to coil it ready for use. She decided to stay there so that I was able to relish my first excursion down the Cut on a pair of narrowboats sitting in comparative comfort on the back end of the butty well-deck. Not for long!

'Take the short shaft to the front. There's a bad bend ahead and you give the bows an extra shove to get them round.'

Reluctantly I moved. I had been enjoying the privilege of gliding through the back gardens of Regent's Park Zoo and the leisure to gaze at the elegant Regency houses on the far side of the towpath. Daphne didn't talk and had her back to me as she steered the boats so that my few minutes of peace had been perfect. Now I would have to join Bash. She squatted on the deck staring ahead and ignored me. The antipathy was mutual.

'Sorry about the rope,' I offered, although there could have been no contrition in the tone of my voice.

'Bloody wet,' she commented. There seemed to be nothing more to say. I could see the bend ahead, and the engine's revs had slowed. I stood there, poised for action, the short shaft (six feet or more in length) held fiercely like a harpoon. There was a swish of water, a spurt on the engine as the boats slowly began to turn through a right-angled bend under a bridge. I looked back at Daphne, who was moving the tiller from side to side in a rowing motion further to aid the turn of the boats. Bash continued to sit. She must be cold. It was her first day as well.

'All right,' called Daphne. 'No need to push. They're round. Come back, both of you. Heads,' she shouted.

The boats slid through the bridge as we ducked instinctively with only inches and seconds to spare. The hazards of life on the boats were becoming obviously ominous during those first hours aboard. Bash and I returned to the security of Daphne's control and expertise. Her reassurance was not entirely reassuring! She told us that there were three downhill locks ahead but that she hoped a lock-keeper would be there to help. We were to be sure to do exactly as he told us!

The canal is wide on this stretch where there is now a thriving youth club afloat on a converted barge flying the Jolly Roger and with a flotilla of canoes and home-made rafts. Then, it was completely deserted and isolated behind the faceless walls of warehouses on one side and the wall beyond the towpath on the other.

The boats slid quietly up to the barrier of the closed gates across the canal. This was our first lock and I, for one, was completely ignorant of the procedure which would enable the boats to reach the level of water which stretched below. Daphne had checked the boats with a burst on the engine in reverse – our only form of brakes – and was scanning the banks of the then unpopulated canal while the traffic on Camden High Road roared away over the bridge beyond the lock.

Daphne kept the boats idling in the channel with the bows just nudging the closed gates.

'Hold them back,' called the man who had appeared on the towpath below the lock. 'Miss French, is it? Heard you were coming through with three new 'uns. Guessed you might need a hand.'

The three 'new 'uns' stood around waiting for instructions. Mary and Bash were detailed to open and shut gates and I was to stay on the butty to watch out for the cill. Completely ignorant of what and why I was to watch, I kept my eyes glued to the back end of the boat which Daphne had indicated and then, as the boats sank with the outflow of water, I saw the cause for possible concern. A stone ledge appeared at the base of the lock behind the boats. This was the 'cill', a platform from which to effect repairs to gates and even boats as the stern of a boat could be allowed to rest on the cill as the lock emptied for inspection of the propeller and the shafting. This was possible only with empty boats, as we were to learn much later in the continual additions to our store of expertise. Meanwhile I soon began to appreciate that Daphne's injunction to watch the butty 'ellum was well justified. As I saw the edge of the cill appear through the sinking level of the water, I realized that the great wooden rudder which projected further than the smaller steel one on the motor could become lodged on the ledge below, with what consequences I was uncertain. I was about to voice my apprehension when Daphne gave the gear-wheel a couple of turns so that the boats slid forwards to the front of the lock so that the rudder was clear of the menacing cill. She turned and smiled, a cigarette dangling.

'These locks have plenty of length,' she explained as she saw that I had understood the possible danger. 'In some of the smaller locks, like those on the Oxford, you have to tie the rudder sideways to make sure it doesn't catch.'

'Back,' called the man from the top of the lock, and again the gearwheel turned to take the boats back against the now visible cill so that the great gates could be swung inwards to the open position. We were now on the lower level of water. Our first lock had been negotiated.

There followed a succession of opening and closing gates, of winding up the paddle gear and learning how to release the safety catch and twist the windlass off the spindle so that the ratchet rattled back down into position. These days lock-keepers seem to insist that the gear be wound back down with the windlass – perhaps for safety reasons. The downward rattle of the paddles was a familiar sound to us when boats were around.

There were moments of near panic for me in one of the locks when Daphne told me to take over while she disappeared down into the cabin for yet another cigarette. As the walls of the lock grew deeper, the boats began to drift backwards. What was I supposed to do?

'A couple of turns to the right on the wheel,' called Daphne. With nervous haste I clutched at the iron gearwheel with both hands and turned it fiercely – too fiercely, as the boats shot forwards with the front fenders hitting the gates.

'Easy now, easy,' called the lock-keeper from above. 'Back into neutral.'

Where on earth was neutral? Daphne came to the rescue.

'Slowly, not so hard . . . listen to the revs . . . watch the water below the counter . . . ease the wheel back the other way.'

I got the feel of it as I reversed the gearwheel and the boats were nudged back by the opening gates. The other two were kept busy with the gates and the winding under the watchful eye of the lock-keeper – his name was Ben. Daphne offered him a cigarette which he tucked behind an ear, saying that he would keep it for later. Cigarettes were on ration but Daphne had a brother in South Africa who kept her well supplied. Even at her present ripe old age of almost eighty, she still smokes twenty a day!

The afternoon was slipping fast into the dusk of an early autumn evening as we negotiated the last lock. Ben had disappeared and Daphne said that she hoped we'd be able to get through the tunnel and tie up below City Road; it seemed that we'd not make the docks until the next day.

They had all stepped off at the last lock, Daphne included. Panic again as I was left 'in charge'.

'Just remember to keep the boats forwards,' said Daphne as she closed the gate on her side and went for'ard to wind up a paddle. Mary and Bash worked as a pair but I noticed that it was Mary who struggled with the winding-gear while Bash stood watching. She had left her windlass on the cabin top of Cleopatra and I was too glued to the gearwheel of the motor to reach it for her.

'Jump down,' Daphne called to Bash as the boats dropped downwards from the edge of the lock. 'Both of you.'

Mary came first, landing lightly on the cabin roof between the water jug and the coil of rope. Bash sat on the stone coping and just managed to slide down with a helping hand from Mary. She'd never make a boatwoman, I thought: too heavy and with no spring. Daphne opened the gates and I slowly edged the boats forwards out of the lock, well pleased with my efforts.

'Hold on,' said the trainer. 'I didn't tell you to go ahead. We have to single out the boats here ready for the tunnel. You weren't to know' – she noted my discomfiture and the smirk on Bash's face.

'Can you get ashore?' she asked as she herself dropped down to the cabin top. The boats were halfway out of the lock as I nodded and edged along the gunwale until I could step off.

'Round to the butty side,' she called as she took the boats back into the back of the lock. The instructions followed fast. 'Mary, undo the cotton line,' and she pointed to the rope holding the sterns of the two boats together. 'Bash, you go up for'ard and untie the bows. Then get on to the motor and come back here. Mary, throw the end of the cotton line up to Margaret, the looped end.'

I managed to catch it, waited for the next instruction. How could one person remember so many details and in their proper sequence *and* organize three such very raw recruits?

'A small metal stud. By the gate, your side. Loop the cotton line over it. Mary, pull it tight and make a figure of eight on the stud behind you. Just a single turn to keep the butty back while I go ahead with the motor. Flick it off the stud on the bank when I wave. Margaret, can you get on board? Leave the gates.'

I dropped down onto the limited space, narrowly missing the windlass Bash had left lying near the water jug. I was the one to flick off the cotton line as Mary was detailed to go to the bows of the butty to help fix the short cross straps, after which she crossed over to the motor and disappeared with Bash into the cabin.

'Leave the tiller,' called Daphne as I had started to heave the wooden arm into place. 'No need to steer with the boats tied close. Make yourself a sandwich. See if the headlight is working – for the tunnel. The switch is just inside – on your left.' I groped around and found a small metal switch. 'Working. Cotton line – quick.'

The line was slipping and straining with the movement of the boats being slowly propelled by the flow of water. A hitch tie would have been disastrous, I thought, as I speedily unwound the two turns Mary had taken round the stud and flicked the loop from the small stud on the bank. The boat gave a lurch as Daphne slowly put the motor ahead.

'All right?' called Daphne. 'Must get on – tunnel. Put some coal on the fire.' I waved at her last instruction as she turned to give her full attention to the business of steering.

I stayed outside for a minute or so to savour more fully the thrill of moving along this ribbon of water through the backstreets of the city. High walls with faceless windows were blanked out by dirt-encrusted glass. Some of the glass was broken to reveal only more encrusted gloom of some interior. What went on behind such walls, such windows? There was almost a total silence behind the distant roar of the traffic, and even that was sporadic now that darkness threatened, when all lights would have to be extinguished. Nightly raids by aircraft and the flying bombs were beginning to sap the life and energy of the City so that in early evening all activity retreated behind the million acres of black-out material.

It would be almost dark before we reached the tunnel, and dark before we tied up and could relax after our first day aboard. The chill of the day struck through my surmisings as the warmth from the range drew me down into the shelter of the cabin. Coal. What had she said about the coal? Where was it? The box on which I was perched. I pulled it out and used my hands to pick out the knobs of coal; it seemed easier than trying to bury the shovel into the awkwardness of the box. The kettle was softly boiling and I thought I might make myself a mug of cocoa. Daphne had told me to make a sandwich, hadn't she? I was always hungry. The cocoa would take the edge off my hunger until supper. I wondered vaguely about the routine of meals; when did we have dinner? Bash had eaten those eccles cakes as if she hadn't eaten for hours. I was soon to realize that her appetite outstripped even my own. Meanwhile, cocoa. I found the tin easily enough in the forefront of the table-cupboard and with a tin of carnation milk already pierced for using.

I had just mixed the creamy, frothing drink when there was a sudden lurch which sent the cocoa slopping over the floor, slightly scalding one of my feet. The whine of the engine registered that it was in reverse and, as I looked out through the hatchway, I saw that the bank opposite was stationary. What was wrong? Still holding the remains of my drink, I climbed out.

The tunnel was just ahead and we had not made it in time. The dreaded timber barge was stuck firmly in the entrance while a solid, patient horse leaned heavily on a line to the fore-end of the wide barge piled high with timber. There were men everywhere shouting instructions back into the darkness of the tunnel mouth.

'You'll have to offload. Too much on. Told you.'

'You'll have to wait, missus,' another shouted at us. 'Better tie up. We'll not get this shifted tonight.'

'You better 'ad – there's muck barges due up tomorrow early.'

I saw Ben, the friendly lock-keeper, arrive on the scene. 'They're sending a tug,' I heard him say.

'Something on the bottom – a barrel most likely. Get another line out. Try to winch her through.'

Meanwhile Daphne took the boats forward again but this time headed for the bank on the offside until the motor effectively was braked by the pile-up of mud. The stern of the butty was skewed round into the channel, vulnerable if the timber barge should come free.

'Get the long shaft and push the stern over,' called Daphne. Carefully I made my way over the cabin top and lowered myself down to the edge of the bunker which took up the width of the boat at the back end of the cabin. It was piled high with barely distinguishable objects, a bicycle being the most prominent, but the centre was clear, with a plank to bridge the gap. The shaft, more than twice as long as myself, was lying along the planks which spanned the empty hold.

'Easier from the cabin roof,' called Daphne as she edged around the gunwale to the engine-room. The engine died as I heaved myself and the awkward length of the shaft to the cabin top, but by then the butty stern had begun to swing back in line with the motor so that my puny efforts to find some leverage in the thick soup of mud below served only to create muddy swirls in the water, while I almost overbalanced as I tried to wrench the shaft back onto the boat. The muddy water dripped along my arms and onto my hand-knitted cardigan. I swung the wretched shaft over into the hold and let it fall where it would, then dropped down through the hatch to the cabin where I stripped off the cardigan and groped in the drawer for my only thick pullover. Suddenly all my clothes seemed thin and inadequate as I pulled on my old, well-worn gaberdine mac. I emerged once more to see what was happening. Nothing. There was no one visible on the Capricorn. Mary and Bash had closed the doors of their cabin, and thick smoke issued from the chimney. I thought I could smell cooking! Presumably Daphne was still in the engine-room. The men on the bank were grouped together, one or two lighting up their seemingly endless supply of 'fags'. I perched on the stern end of the Cleopatra and waited in case I should be needed. Last night, I reflected, I was talking with Kay and Frances at Joe's over a frugal farewell supper with lots of 'coffee' and lots of talk. I was glad to be away, to be sitting on the back end of a boat so near and yet so removed from the noise and the talking . . . the endless talking.

The horse was still, a darkening shape in the growing darkness, and I wondered what the next move would be. Would we have to stay here as one of the men had said? There was nowhere to tie the boats, and the thought of spending the night marooned in a sea of mud was not an attractive prospect despite the fact that we were separated from the grass-fringed wall of a building by only a few feet. It was better to tie up on the offside if possible, Daphne had told me at Maida Vale, so that we would not obstruct any lines from horse-drawn barges; also it was safer from any hooligans who might be attracted to the boats if tied on the towpath side. The men continued to smoke and to talk among themselves, seemingly uninterested in the problem of the barge wedged in the mouth of the tunnel ahead. I wondered idly what would happen if another barge should come up behind it but then realized how obvious it would be to any steerer that the road was blocked: the half circle of light ahead would be blocked out.

I saw Daphne's head emerge from the side doors of the engine-room and then withdraw. What could she be doing? I began to scribble some notes into my diary about procedures for taking the boats through downhill locks and was considering making myself a sandwich when another sound caught my attention.

A small tug appeared, going astern with a belching exhaust which a slight breeze carried straight towards the Cleopatra. The black smuts danced and settled on the cabin roof, and a sudden sting in my eye caused pain and discomfort for the next hour or so. The men on the bank moved slowly, drew on their fags and set about to renew their efforts to free the barge. A couple of lines from the stern of the tug were made fast to the bows of the barge by a shapeless shape dimly outlined against the timber. My eye was hurting and watering but I was glued to the action.

'Right . . . NOW . . .' The order was shouted from another shape on the towpath. Even more smoke poured from the exhaust as the lines tautened. The horse slipped and heaved, and the flints from its hooves spat into the darkening air like fireflies.

Slowly, like a cork being drawn, the great, wide barge slid out from the circle of darkness. I was terrified of its bulk – the canal suddenly seemed so narrow; but it passed us easily, with several feet to spare. A stocky man with a shapeless hat pulled down over his ears leaned on the great tiller – a hunk of wood thrust through a roughly cut groove at the head of the massive rudder.

'All clear now,' he shouted cheerfully. I was conscious of the grit in my eye and only nodded in reply.

Daphne re-emerged from the engine-room. 'All right to go through?' she called to Ben, who was leaning on his bike.

'I'll close up behind you,' he called in reply. 'Nothing else coming up.'

'Bash, come and help me start up,' called Daphne, knocking on the cabin side. Slowly and with extreme care, Bash edged herself round to the engine-room, and a moment later the heavy thump of the diesel engine brought the boats to life again. There seemed to be nothing I could do, and the smell of bacon from the motor cabin reminded me of my own hunger but it would seem churlish now not to wait for Daphne. How much longer, I wondered, before we would stop for the night? So much for a nine-to-five day! Daphne was pushing the stern of the motor away from the bank with the short shaft pronged into the grass verge. It was hard work with the weight of the butty still attached to the stern.

'I'll loose you off,' she called to me. 'Can you come up to the front and shaft the bows over so that I can pick you up when I'm free?' (The 'I' was synonymous with the boat!)

She loosed off the straps from the motor stern and, without the encumbrance, the motor slid easily astern and into the channel, although the wash only seemed to push the butty even further into the mud. Wearily I again clambered over the cabin roof, retrieved the length of shaft and made my way to the end of the planks where the structure of the cratch obstructed access to the foredeck. My eye was closed and watering against the prick of the grit and my arms ached as I manœuvred the muddy shaft to find a purchase against the bank. The old mac would protect my only thick pullover from the mud; I realized already that the mac was doomed to be ruined. I leaned with all my puny weight upon the shaft until, gradually, I felt the bows shift from the bed of mud. Meanwhile Daphne had eased the motor ahead.

'Think you can get round the fore-end to give me the straps?' she called.

I was too tired to answer, threw the shaft back into the hold regardless of the splash of mud across the front of my mac, threw my arms around the tent-like structure of the cratch, clutching at the top strings, and edged my way to the front deck. I was beyond caring whether or not I went overboard. Why couldn't Mary or Bash come to help?

'You all right?' asked Daphne as I handed her the two short straps.

'Grit in my eye.'

'Bash and Mary are very tired. I told them to get supper.'

My unreason refused and resented the excuse. They couldn't possibly feel more tired than myself.

'Can you steer the butty through the tunnel?' Daphne continued. 'To stop the stern from scraping.' I was beginning to dislike the soft, yet decisive voice with its endless stream of instructions, directed, I thought irrationally, at only myself.

'Not far now,' said the voice reassuringly. 'Take down the chimney.'

Wearily I clambered back to the shelter of the well-deck, heaved the wooden tiller into its slot and drooped limply across the support of its length. My undue weariness was due partly to hunger. I had eaten only an apple and a piece of cake since breakfast. The tea and the half-mug of cocoa had revived me at the time but now there was a gnawing hole in my gut and a great lassitude through my whole body. Take down the chimney, had she said? I gripped the black painted chimney pot with both hands, not at all certain just how I should take it down. Luckily it wasn't too hot, just delightfully warm to my mud-encrusted hands. There was only one way to dislodge the thing – upwards. It moved and, as I jerked it again, it came free of the supporting collar. Luckily again it was held by a supporting chain set into a metal ring on the cabin roof or it might well have gone overboard. I dropped it hastily as a funnel of black smoke poured from the hole just below the level of my face. A gust from the tunnel blew it directly backwards before I could step sideways out of its track. Both eyes were now completely closed as I dropped the chimney.

I felt streaked with mud, with smoke and with weariness. I don't remember the short passage through the tunnel; perhaps I dozed!

Suddenly the revs ahead changed to a quiet idling sound and I opened my eyes. I was surprised that the banks and the buildings were still quite visible in the long hours of an early autumn dusk which always seem to stretch into the daylight and far into the night darkness ahead, especially on the canals, where shadows and shapes take on a numinous light from the gleam of the water.

'Going in here,' Daphne called to me as she opened the doors of the motor cabin. 'Mary and Bash, come and help.'

We were going in alongside a cinder path edged by a stone coping and backed by tall blank walls which isolated us from the on-going life on the further side. I saw Bash pick up the short shaft and make her way round the gunwale, along the top planks to the fore-end. Mary stood perched on the narrow gunwale, both waiting for instructions. I continued to droop over the tiller. Daphne gave a short burst astern so that the motor drew in neatly to lie alongside the bank. Bash jumped off heavily with the shaft, with which she pulled the length of rope attached to the stud on the bows.

'Don't pull it in,' shouted Daphne as she stepped off herself with a line from the stern to prevent it swinging out. 'Take out the tiller and get off if you can,' she called back to me. She had to think for everyone in those early days, to give the instructions and to envisage all the possibilities of mistaken enthusiasm which could so easily foul up even the simplest manœuvre. I struggled with the heavy curved tiller and perched it on the step between the open cabin doors. The stern was beginning to swing away from the bank. I should have called to Mary or Daphne and thrown a rope across. But no! I had to step up onto the deck side, rope in hand, and take a flying leap to the receding bank. Of course I missed and was down over my head into the black, cold water. Instinctively I kicked my way upwards and grabbed at the sides of the coping. Mary stood there looking at me helplessly while I tried to find a toehold. I was still holding the rope and shouted at her to take it.

'Put it through a ring and tie it.'

'She's gone in,' said Bash cheerfully as Daphne joined them.

'Don't pull on that rope,' she said briskly, 'or the stern will hit her,' and indeed, the high black sides of the hull loomed ominously close.

There must have been many others before and since who have experienced the difficulty of scrambling out from the depth of water with no foothold or handhold in the smooth concreted sides of the bank. Bash and Daphne tried to heave but my clothes were waterlogged and I hung there heavily; the mac didn't help! I had been scrabbling with my toes in the old plimsolls I was wearing and then found a break or protuberance in the smooth surface; anyway it was just enough to give me the necessary purchase on which to push as they pulled. I floundered like a wet seal onto the grime of the path.

'Engine-room and strip off,' said Daphne.

The engine-room was warm, and lines were strung across it for the purpose of drying clothes. Daphne brought me in some pieces of underwear, a pair of trousers and one of her own pullovers.

'Couldn't find another one in your drawer,' she commented. I hadn't another!

'A good start,' she said briefly and I felt suitably ashamed of my own stupidity.

I had struggled out of the sodden mac, now well grimed with cinders and mud which the immersion had done nothing to cleanse but rather had saturated the filth into the very fabric so that it would always remain a shapeless and grimy garment. As such it was to be invaluable, no longer proofed against the rain but unaffected by further exposure to mud and oil and the grime of ropes and locksides. I hung it on a convenient hook and began to towel my face and hair – streaked and gritty.

Daphne withdrew and the tears spilled over. What a day! What a mess I had made of everything. How Bash would be grinning over my stupidity. No doubt she would be saying, 'Serve her bloody well right – gives herself such airs.' I knew this and continued to weep tears of mortification as I stripped and shivered. No good being sorry for myself. I had to return to the cabin and to the censure of Daphne's criticism; I didn't even have that extra pullover and would have to borrow hers until mine was dry. I couldn't see whether or not the dirt had seeped through to my skin and there was no kind of a mirror to reflect back the unlovely image of myself so that I hastily scrambled into the comforting warmth of dry clothes. No socks or shoes; my feet were frozen.

I gulped back my wretchedness and clambered out of the engine-room. Should I close the doors? Every move in this unknown territory was fraught with uncertainty. My bare feet clamped onto the narrow gunwale and I gripped fiercely with my hands the ridged coping of the butty cabin. There was no sound from either cabin as I clambered across to the butty. Both hatches and doors were closed against the darkness so that no lights were visible.

'All right to come in?' I called, my voice high with apprehension.

One side of the door was pushed open from the inside.

'Come in quickly. The light . . .' said Daphne. I almost fell into the cabin, eager to ingratiate myself.

'Slippers?' asked Daphne.

'Thick socks in my drawer.' Slippers were an unessential luxury in my meagre wardrobe. I noticed that Daphne was wearing warm and serviceable-looking felt ones.

The cabin was warm and cheerful in the soft light from the fifteen-amp bulb. Daphne had made another pot of tea and had boiled a couple of precious eggs.

'Never take risks,' she said as I sipped the hot tea. 'An accident of working boats is a liability. Not that you could have known, of course,' she added kindly in response to my crestfallen silence. Of course I should have known. How on earth could I have been so stupid? What had happened to all my training on the Return? My leap from the gunwale had only served to push the stern even further from the bank. I thought I had learned that lesson from sailing days when I had been immersed more than once trying to bridge the gap between boat and a receding bank.

The boiled egg choked in my throat as I fought with my emotions. I was tired and completely deflated. With all the fresh air, with the complete change of environment and the strangeness of strangers with whom I would have to live and work so closely, and with the shock of my sudden immersion I was exhausted and wanted only to retreat into a corner and to howl my eyes out. I had left behind me the security of my own room, my own books and few possessions, the friends with whom I had shared heartbreaks and hopes, the career in which I had begun to enjoy the early taste of success; and I had stepped sideways into a completely different way of life, with other kinds of people drawn to a nomadic existence on the waterways possibly for reasons as nebulous and tentative as my own.

I concentrated on sipping my tea as I struggled to regain some semblance of composure. Daphne wisely continued with her own meal in silence.

At that time in my life I was in a highly neurotic state and was over-sensitive to any implied criticism and with every failure on my part to achieve perfection. Later on I was to meet others like myself and to recognize the symptoms which drove ourselves and those with whom we worked to exhaustion and beyond, with our exacting standards of efficiency and perfection. It was only when I did become an efficient boatman that I learned to relax and to laugh at the incidents so often caused by lack of concentration and experience. What had we been trying to prove to ourselves? Was there over-compensation for past failure or disappointment? Was there, in those far-off days, a deep-seated feminine need to assert ourselves, to be 'as good as the men' and even better? There was the obvious need to be accepted by the boatpeople themselves and on their terms; to sustain and survive the rigours of the work and not to be one of the many drop-outs who did not survive even the six weeks of training.

I think back on some of them who did survive (*see* Pl. 3). There was Helen Skyrme, small, feminine and elegant, who later told me that she had been appalled by the conditions of living and working but who had thought 'If they can do it, so can I' and I'm sure she never regretted the challenge. There was Margery, who earned the reputation of driving herself and her crews to such an extent that few stayed to crew with her for more than a couple of trips. There was the Audrey, Evelyn and Anne team, old-timers who had reached pinnacles of perfection in the eyes of novices like myself; Olga, who wore strange and erotic gear; Emma Smith who was to write *Maidens' Trip*, the classic of the three books which are rooted in our unique experience; and Susan Blood, Susan Woolfitt, Virginia Shadwell; Cecily, a foot-loose New Zealander who was working her way around the world unde-terred by such hindrances as wars in Europe and the Far East; Pat, who came to escape from the problems of an 'innocent' and inescapable pregnancy; Madge and Averil, who had lived and worked on the Alphons, my present home now converted into a state of comfort and luxury; Kay, a teacher like myself; the indomitable Elsie, a dressmaker from somewhere in the East End of London, for whom Daphne's word was absolute law; the strange character of Jo; Sonia, who was to marry George and then the late Tommy Rolt; Stella and Christian on the Hyperion which, later, I was to take over.

There were the two trainers, Kit Gayford and Daphne French, who not only displayed vast resources of patience and endurance to teach the skills to many who would stay on the boats for only a week or two, maybe for a few months, but who also had to cope with all the varying quirks of personality and background of the continuing trickle of aspiring trainees who came to join the boats.

Success for us who stayed, as a group of women and aliens, was essential if we were to be treated by the boatpeople as serious contributors to the canal trade. Reputations on the Cut were established slowly and based upon our own attitudes to the work and to our proper regard for the ways and taboos established by the boatpeople over the decades. To be over-familiar with the men, to peer into cabins, even to lean against another's boat, to pass across the stern of a boat by the cabin instead of across the bows at the far end (and even then you were expected to ask permission from the steerer or his mate), to leave paddles raised and gates open so that pounds were drained, to neglect the use of sideponds when emptying or filling a lock; in fact, to infringe any of the countless unwritten laws of the Cut was to evoke ridicule and antagonism from those upon whose goodwill and help our survival depended. Gradually over the weeks and months, as we grew to think of ourselves as boatwomen, we accepted the codes of conduct for our own so that even now, almost forty years later, I bristle with impotent anger at the constant infringement of even the most self-evident rules for the proper use of the canals and resent those who have no love or care for such a valuable inheritance from the eighteenth and nineteenth centuries, no interest or admiration for such originators as the Duke of Bridgewater, Brunel and Telford, and who so often abuse the freedom from constraints still to be enjoyed along the great network of navigable waterways in our small island.

To return to that first evening aboard the Cleopatra: the hot tea, the warmth of the cabin and Daphne's easy disregard of my dejection gradually restored my deflated optimism. A bad start, as she had said, but I had learned the hard way that prudence on the boats was preferable to displays of athletic gymnastics. As I managed to choke down the precious egg, Daphne started to talk about sailing. She had her own boat, the Embla, laid up for the war years in Cork harbour. As she talked in her soft and delicate voice, I recovered completely and joined in with my own anecdotes of holidays on the Return.

'The boat was so precious,' I said, 'and I inherited the tradition of putting the safety of the boat first and myself second. I was the fender between Yarmouth quay and the precious side of the boat many a time.'

'Not on these boats,' said Daphne. 'Your own safety comes first. These boats are strong and can take a few knocks.'

I had thawed out physically and emotionally and, when the washing up was done and the beds were ready, slept into oblivion.

We came down to Limehouse early the following morning. A night of dreamless and untroubled sleep had completely restored my optimism and revived my spirits.

3. Training Boats: First Trip

I thumb through the closely written pages of my old diary to re-savour those early impressions of my first trip down to Regent's Canal dock and read:

4 September

We started at 6.30 a.m. and came through the heart of London, past enormous and mysterious factories, timberyards, warehouses. I thought of all the people still sleeping, beginning to shake out of sleep by the clanging of endless alarmclocks, heavy and unlovely in the morning grope for tea and hot water. How could they even guess at our myth-like existence as we slid past their grimed windows and their pathetic little gardens . . .

I was so arrogant in the pleasure of my separate existence! I wonder at the 6.30 a.m. start! Daphne must have had orders for loading that morning and wanted to be sure of not missing her turn. No one chose to stay longer than was absolutely necessary on that pond of water locked in by the high concrete walls. There were nights when the rumble of planes overhead and the nearby barking of the ack-ack guns made us feel horribly vulnerable in our small boats, so that we were glad to be loaded and off again to the comparative safety of the countryside.

The stream of slim boats slid in and out of London through some of the heaviest raids and scenes of destruction, yet only one pair in all that time was ever really damaged, and even then there was no loss of life. Kit's boats were shocked by blast but luckily they were out of the basin and into the narrow canal, and no real damage was done. I remember thinking that I felt safer on the boats than ever I would have done evacuated to some distant outpost in the Welsh mountains!

However, it seems that we were not loaded that day, as my old journal has an entry for the following day which records my first impressions of the dock. The coastal traffic on which we depended for our cargoes had become extremely sporadic and unpredictable so that boats and crews could wait for as long as a week tied up within the confines of the basin. There were three other pairs waiting for loads, and we were all tied together end-on to the high wall of the dock like some gaily painted pontoon bridge across which Daphne made her way – across the bows away from the cabins! – to the iron-runged ladder set into the concrete. She disappeared over the top into an amalgam of sheds, cranes, piles of rusty iron rods and anonymous-looking crates. The other two had not emerged and I was left to tidy up the cabin while Daphne had gone to find out when we might hope to be loaded. I had precious moments to myself in which to write up more of those early impressions.

5 September
We are anchored [I still retained my sailing terminology!] in Lime-house dock. From the cabin I can see the silhouettes of gigantic cranes, the darker blur of warehouses and sheds, and further over in the basin the grey hulls of other barges and ships – real sea-going ships – waiting to offload their cargoes, some of which we might carry to Birmingham or Coventry. There is a wind blowing so that the boat moves slightly and there is a soft lapping under the stern and against the sides. We are in the heart of London with a war raging about us and yet what peace there is in this small cabin. Timber barges, horses, uphill and downhill locks, lock-keepers, the exchange of good coal for tins of sardines, wind and rain – my first day as a bargee! This life is strangely different from anything that most people whom I know could imagine . . .

How naïve I was and what a romantic simpleton!

Daphne returned with the news that we were to be loaded with iron rods to Tyseley.

'Rotten cargo. They'll shift,' she said but we could get loaded at once if we'd take them. The other boats were waiting for the coaster to offload crates of tinned meat. 'We could be lucky,' she said with a grin. 'Now, the oranges.'

Mary and Bash had joined us to know what was happening. Daphne told us to get all the containers we could find. A crate of oranges had broken and we could help ourselves.

We had almost forgotten the taste of an orange and lost no time in gathering up bags, rucksack and even a bucket. We made our way up the ladder and joined in the free-for-all on the dockside. There was an enormous wooden vat partly filled with the errant fruit, and more oranges were rolling about on the floor of the shed where the crates were being stacked. Such riches! Greedily we staggered back to the boats laden with as many as we could carry. By the end of that trip I never wanted to see or to smell another orange! Daphne's brother had sent her a large consignment of sugar and throughout that trip every spare moment was spent down in the cabin cutting and chopping and squeezing the endless supply of oranges to make marmalade, which must have lasted until peace finally was declared. It was all cooked in small amounts on the top of the range, no pan being large enough to take more than two or three pounds at a time; and it constantly had to be stirred to prevent the bubbling mess sticking – no teflon or stick-proof pans in those days! We begged for jamjars all along the route, and when the last orange had been cooked or eaten, the space under the side-bed was almost filled with our cost-free store.

'Ready there, Capricorn?' called a man from the side as we dumped the oranges into the butty cabin.

The next two hours were spent in shifting the planks to free the hold, shifting the boats into position for the crane to deposit the bundles of rods which tipped the boats alarmingly as they were released, and finally shifting the planks back into position along the centre lengths of the boats.

'Chains and sidecloths next,' said Daphne when the final bundle of rods had been lowered.

The boats were now low down in the water, although the rods

filled only half the available space. From her store of 'treasures' in the bunker Daphne retrieved two short pieces of metal similar to the rods with which we were loaded. There were three sets of chains along each side of the boats which were joined across the hold with large bolts screwed together and tightened with the aid of the improvised levers. These chains pulled in the sides of the hulls to keep them from expansion with the bulk of the cargo; an extra width of even an inch or so could be enough to wedge the boats in some of the narrower locks. The top planks were now elevated upon vertical struts along the lengths of the holds and bolted into position at the height of the cabin tops. They had to be held firmly as so often they were used as access from one end of the boat to the other. Then came the side-cloths – grease-impregnated and rolled along the length of each gunwale. 'Good for your hands,' commented Daphne as we grimaced and unrolled them to release the top strings, which were pulled upwards and over the top planks to stretch the sidecloths tautly, affording protection of the cargo from any possible inrush of water in a lock or from a possible jolt of the boats.

'No topcloths,' continued Daphne as we ruefully surveyed broken nails and oily streaks. 'We might need to shift those rods. Hope it doesn't rain.'

It did rain, as my journal records: *'Today we came back from Limehouse through blinding rain which did nothing to dampen my enthusiasm. The difference between this and teaching is incredible – and amazingly good.'*

Finally we were off, through the lock and back into the canal. I was slightly disappointed not to have seen more of Limehouse beyond the dock gates but was glad to get away from the dangers of that land-locked basin. We didn't go far and tied up at Salmons Lane where there was a water tap. Daphne said I might wash my hair! I was reasonably proud of my blonde hair in those days, and it had become streaked with oil and grit from my immersion. No doubt Daphne had taken note of my occasional moan! We all looked wet and bedraggled; the fire in the motor cabin was out and Daphne said we should dry off and come for tea in the butty cabin. Surprisingly it was already tea-time – a four o'clock tea-time; supper would come later. On the training boats we had a midday dinner which consisted mainly of an everlasting stew with potatoes and vegetables all cooked together in the same pan on the range.

Bash had disappeared into the warmth of the engine-room, and Mary was left to organize the motor cabin for the comfort of the evening ahead. Daphne handed her a few dry sticks from the small store under the range shelf and advised her to pick up more as we went along and to dry them off so that there would always be some for fire-lighting. I became a fanatic about collecting sticks so that we always had a plentiful supply – a habit I have retained, although these days the supply is far less plentiful and the number of 'gleaners' has increased. Anyway, I am now less energetic, and the phurnacite 'eggs' are so convenient and give out so much warmth that my scavenging is restricted to keeping a box of sticks ready for re-lighting the Torglow stove.

More tea, and Daphne spread some hunks of bread with peanut butter. There was still plenty of bread available; the rationing was to come later. 'Call them over,' she said as I perched on the step enjoying the rest and the warmth. I had filled the two water cans, and the prospect of a washing session and a relaxed evening ahead lent an extra warmth to the lassitude of tired muscles.

They came over, both dirty and silent. Mary's face and hands were smudged with coal and grime, and her dark blue guernsey had a ragged tear in the sleeve. She brought a pair of socks with her and asked if she could change and dry her shoes by our fire. Bash was still chewing gum as she subsided onto the bench opposite the fire. I had retreated to the back end of the cabin while Mary remained perched on the step in the hatchway. There was a constraint between them; neither spoke after Mary's query. Bash went on chewing and even ignored the pile of peanut-buttered bread in front of her.

As Daphne poured tea, the difficulties of two such disparate persons as Bash and the timid Mary sharing the motor cabin spilled over and, while Daphne offered advice and suggestions, I cravenly crawled under the table flap, past Mary and into the refuge of the engine-room where the pee-bucket was kept. How thankful I was to be sharing with Daphne rather than with Bash or the inadequacies of Mary. I perched on the bucket in the cold blackness and wondered how Bash and Mary would resolve their differences in the weeks ahead. Then the boat lurched and I knew they had returned to their own cabin on the far side of the bulkhead. I called out as I scrambled over to the butty but only Mary answered. Daphne said that I could have the cabin to myself for a strip-wash while she went over to help sort out their living arrangements.

The luxury of a bowl full of hot water replenished from the ever-boiling kettle on the fire in which I washed my hair, my grey and grimy skin and finally my mud-encrusted cardigan, has no equal, in my estimation, in all the modern gadgetry and plumbing aboard the elegant conversions of the old boats. I squeezed out the cardigan and hung it across the brass rail over the range; it would be dry by morning. I got into pyjamas, pullover and socks and proceeded to make our supper of sardines on toast and a jug of cocoa.

'How are they?' I asked when Daphne finally returned.

'Warm and fed,' she replied. 'Beds are the problem. Bash fits into the cupboard but complains that she has to keep her knees bent and that Mary's feet take up all the space. It's difficult when we all seem to be so much larger than the boatpeople.' I too was conscious of sharing the corner with Daphne's feet and had tucked them up out of the way that first night I was aboard. A few more nights of such intimacies and personal considerations were soon forgotten; we were often glad of the extra warmth generated by proximity in the pre-dawn chill of winter mornings.

Refreshed and relaxed, I decided to renew my old habit of a read in bed before sleep. The extra width of my shelf-bed made it possible to have a candle. I tried to organize the flickering light and the thin, inadequate pillow though Daphne warned me that fire was a terrible hazard on the boats. I had brought with me a thick volume of *War and Peace* which I thought would last me for the training trips. Daphne had taken off her glasses, skewered a piece of hair with a grip into the semblance of a curl, slid down into her own cocoon and immediately was breathing softly. My efforts to read and the book I had brought suddenly seemed so pretentious in the simple seclusion of the boatman's cabin that I blew out the candle and listened to the companionable breathing in the dark warmth of my third night aboard. My last conscious thought was that we were complete strangers who would have to live and tolerate each other's differences for at least six weeks in the narrow confines of our travelling home. That was the only time I ever attempted to read in bed on the training boats; I was soon to learn the effects that eight to ten hours of winds and weathers would have upon my sleep patterns.

'Good, the rain has stopped.' Daphne opened a door the next morning to peer out at the weather. I had an extra half hour in the warmth of my bed while she donned pullover and specs and organized the fire and the primus with the top half of her torso while the bottom half remained encased in the blankets. Her movements in the half-light, the gradual smell of warmth and tea which began to penetrate my easeful sloth are among my pleasantest memories of those early days.

It was a quiet autumn day with no wind – an ideal day for travelling and ideal for the novices to be further initiated into the skills of taking a pair of loaded boats back through the locks. Ben reappeared to help us wind the paddles and to add his own instructions and information to that of our trainer.

The boats were singled out with the butty towed on a short strap. Mary and I were on the butty while Bash offered to stay on the towpath to help with the gates and the paddles. They were uphill locks this way, and Daphne took the boats in slowly, throwing off the towing strap from the stud on the motor counter at the precise moment when the butty had enough speed to slide into the lock chamber alongside the motor. Mary took out the tiller immediately the bows drew into the space while I leaped off onto the bank, checking-strap in hand and windlass tucked into the back of my belt. My enthusiasm still outweighed my prudence, and it was a long time before I could emulate the seemingly leisured movements of the boatpeople as they controlled the boats with real efficiency to the extent that violent action was hardly ever required. The long-skirted women would step off from the butty almost elegantly and judge to a nicety the speed of the boat so that an easy turn with the checking-strap around the 'stump' or bollard would allow it to slide into the lock barely grazing the lockside in its progress. At the same time they would often be shouting instructions about the cooking or the cat or the children to someone still down in the cabin. It took a long time for us to acquire this ease and almost nonchalant accuracy of judgement.

I ran up the steps to reach the top of the lock and the 'stump' around which I would have to take a couple of turns with the rope to check the speed of the butty in such a frenzy that I tripped and almost fell. Ben took the strap from me and wound it easily round the bollard.

'Take it easy. More haste, less speed.' He proceeded with his advice as we progressed up to the Old Ford locks where he left us. 'Wind up slowly. Half a paddle first. Don't want to swamp the boats . . . Put your back into it . . . Always make sure the safety catch is on . . . Leave the gates closed – saves the water . . . Check the paddles are down before you leave each lock . . . Watch your iron . . . Dig in your heels to move the gates . . . Could do with some good boots – plimsolls not much good for this sort of work . . . Miss French shown you round Commercial Road? Boots and sailors' gear there without coupons . . . Any spare tins of sardines?'

Daphne had half a dozen tins and a packet of cigarettes ready for him as he prepared to leave but he would take only a couple of tins, saying that we would need them more than he; but he was grateful for the 'fags'.

It was a long day as we travelled back through Acton, the tunnel, Camden and Maida Vale, where I had joined the boats three – or was it four? – days earlier. It seemed like a lifetime, and my previous life as a teacher and a clippie belonged to someone else. Mary and I took turns to jump off and check the butty, while Bash seemed content enough to go ahead lockwheeling. At the Maida Vale tunnel there was a toll office where the trip card was checked and signed and where there was a message for Daphne that we should wait at the Southall depot until Miss Minn arrived.

Then we were off on the four hours of pounding back to Bull's Bridge at Southall. There was no incident and we began to flatter ourselves that we were well on the way to becoming boatwomen!

We continued uneventfully past a cemetery, a golf course and factories where we would offload our cargoes of coal on the return trip, and incongruous stretches of countryside interspersed with blocks of urban development.

'I'll make some tea,' I said to Mary, who seemed content to steer and disinclined to talk. I retreated to the cabin, made up the fire and stretched out on the side-bed with *War and Peace* to wait until the kettle should boil. I must have dozed. The next I knew was Mary's voice calling me to come up. We had arrived at the turn into Bull's Bridge depot – another of those right-angled bends!

We tied up just beyond the school – a boat pulled up on the bank with the hold roofed over to convert the space into a makeshift classroom. The boatchildren attended the school whenever the boats were held up at the depot, a few days at most. It was hardly surprising that most of the boatpeople could neither read nor write, although many of the women could tell to a penny the amount of money that should be in their pay packets. The few children who were literate had been left with shore-based relatives for a year or two so that they could attend school on a more regular basis.

'Never told them we were off the boats though,' one of these boatwomen told me later, 'or they'd call us gippos and spit at us – worse sometimes.' I was reminded of the gipsy children who occasionally attended the small country school where I had done some teaching after leaving college. They were always regarded with hostility and suspicion by teachers and parents as well as by the other children, while they in turn were fearful, aggressive and antagonistic to any efforts we might make to initiate them into the mysteries of our 'educational' activities. Their parents came in vans for the strawberry-picking and camped with their dogs on the edge of Holt Forest and, for the few weeks they were there, no one ventured along the lane which led past their camp. Bolt your doors. Don't go out at night. Don't walk to the pub on your own. Keep your dogs tied up. If you don't behave, I'll give you to the gipsies.

As I peered in at the windows of the boat school, I remembered the old warnings with shame and regret. How easy it was to condemn that which was different and unknown. Well, I was one of the 'outsiders' now, a bargee, a water gipsy still regarded with suspicion and disapproval by shopkeepers and by many we met with in pubs along the way.

The office was closed and the workshops were empty; everyone left for home before the black-out.

'We'll have a late start,' said Daphne to me. 'You could nip back to your room in Chelsea if you like. I'll have to wait for Miss Minn in the morning.'

I went, phoned a couple of friends and we all met at Student Movement House, where I swaggered about in my trousers and pullover and bragged about the hazards of being a bargee! At the same time, how I relished the hot bath, the privacy of my own room and the comfort of my own bed! However, I was awake at 6 a.m. and ready to return. Daphne had said I should be back by 9 a.m. but when I reached the boats she was still in bed. I made the tea and asked after the other two.

'Not too good,' she sighed. 'They're so different. Mary's willing enough but really rather helpless, and Bash enjoys bullying her. I had them in for supper and Bash ate through all our meat ration – sorry! Mary ate hardly anything. Don't know how it will work out.'

As it happened, the difficulties of the motor cabin were resolved with the arrival of Miss Minn. She called Daphne over to the paint shop and then Daphne returned to the motor cabin where I heard her call for Mary. 'Bring your holdall,' I heard her say. They rejoined Miss Minn and then the three of them went to a taxi that was waiting behind the office. That was the last we saw of Mary and, guessing at explanations, I thought she must have suffered a shock – an accident to relatives or a friend perhaps.

Daphne returned looking sombre. She called to Bash to come and join us for breakfast, when she would explain. I emptied a couple of tins of baked beans into a saucepan and, as I stirred the beans, I thought that it could be an easier trip with only two novices for Daphne to watch. It seemed that Mary had been wrongly discharged from a mental home. She had suicidal tendencies and had been in care since she cut her wrists a year ago. We were shocked by the news and drew closer as a wave of sympathy for the quiet, withdrawn girl swept over us.

We were very subdued. What were our own problems by comparison? Later on there was to be Harold, the poor, frightened boy who invented a kindly grandmother for himself; there was Jo, who was to join our boats in Coventry – a person torn by conflicts, doubts and terrors. And now there was Mary, another refugee from the threats and anxieties of capricious relationships who had thought to find on the boats an escape from the trap sprung to ensnare the years of her youth. They were all victims of circumstance with never a hope of redressing such an imbalance of problems which already had destroyed any possibility for success and content in their lives. I knew only a small number of the trainees with any degree of intimacy but it seemed that many of us were on the Cut to escape from problems and difficulties with which life 'out there' had confronted us. We were too young (despite my twenty-eight years!), too ignorant, perhaps too idealistic and vulnerable to realize or accept that there was no escape. Like Mary and Jo and Harold, our problems were part of us and our only chance for survival lay in acceptance and compromise. Did Mary ever succeed in coming to terms with so many adverse influences in her young life? I have often wondered but remain doubtful. It was evident in the short time that she was with us that the tough streak of survival which drives most to continue, almost despite the odds, in her was febrile and hesitant. Her shadow lay heavily over all of us.

'We'll get going,' said Daphne briefly.

The three of us set out for Tyseley, Bash and I on the butty, Daphne on the motor. After Cowley Bash and I would take turns on the motor, with Daphne standing on the gunwale to salvage results of misjudgements and to continue with the endless instructions and information of which we were so ignorant.

The hard physical work helped to ease our thoughts. I found that my own neurotic tendencies to introspection were reduced almost to extinction by the demands made upon judgement and concentration. The co-ordination of mind and body which improved gradually as the days passed was intensely satisfying. The more proficient I became, the more I began to enjoy and exhilarate in the present instead of being torn by past unhappiness and disappointment and being obsessed with senseless anxieties about an unpredictable future.

On the way to Cowley I attempted to reach over the gulf which separated Bash and myself. She steered while I peeled potatoes, carrots and onions; later I would add a tin of 'bully' to the veg broth.

'What's your real name?' I asked. 'I can't go on calling you Bash.'

She didn't see why not, as that was what she was called at home. She had six brothers and had earned her 'moniker' the hard way. Then, offhandedly, she told me that her name was Peggy. I firmly used her real name after that, and I think she liked me the better for it.

It had been thought at the Ministry that recruits from the tougher districts of London might prove more suitable for work on the boats than those from the professional and leisured classes who, until then, had formed the majority of the women trainees, and Peggy was one of the first from the new recruitment drive. After my training I stayed on Capricorn and Cleopatra for a further six months as trainer's mate, and during that period we had a succession of these 'tough' characters. They left even more speedily than those from the more privileged backgrounds, many not completing even the initial training trips.

Peggy joined us in the evenings for supper. It seemed callous to isolate her in the motor cabin; she was a gregarious soul and would have been wretched. As it was, she put off the hour of crossing back to her own cabin until we almost pushed her out. 'The fire's out,' she called out more often than not when we had planned washing sessions or some other domestic occupation which took up the cabin space during the hour or so between supper and bed. Our sympathy dwindled after listening for hours to the endless saga of her exploits to outwit authority at school and in the factory where she had worked.

At Cowley the boats were gauged again and the trip card was signed. 'Nothing been down,' said the lock-keeper. 'Locks will be half empty though. Lot of leaky gates in need of repairs. Forty-two more uphills to the summit. Good exercise.' To me his grin was more than a shade sadistic.

The shallow lock at Uxbridge (four feet seven inches deep) lulled us into a false sense of security and I gasped at the sight of the one by the gravelpit ahead. Denham Deep was well named with a depth of over eleven feet.

'We'll breast the boats up,' called Daphne. I was to go to the front end of the butty and tie the bows of the two boats together when they came alongside each other. Peggy pulled out the butty tiller while I made my way along those top planks – less than a foot wide. But Peggy had withdrawn the tiller too soon so that she could not check the steering, and the butty bows were heading straight for the motor stern as Daphne threw off the towing strap.

'Watch out,' she called but I had seen the inevitable impact and crouched with toes and hands clamped to the planks. Daphne gave a burst to the engine so that the sudden wash partially deflected the oncoming butty, and the crash was reduced to a good nudge and a scrape as the motor went astern and then ahead so that it came, more or less, alongside the butty. The nudge had been sufficient to send the water slopping up over the sides of the butty and I appreciated the protective function of the sidecloths. I clambered down onto the foredeck and managed to lasso the stud on the motor foredeck with the line from the butty. At last the manœuvre known as 'breasting up' was completed and the two boats were neatly tied fore and aft to lie alongside each other. But we were all marooned on the boats, and the formidable gates ahead were blankly closed against us. A small gush of water was spilling through the crack between the gates from about halfway down.

'Have to empty the lock. Can you jump off?' Daphne called to me.

At long last my long legs were to prove their worth! I flew over the gap and landed with ease on the grassy verge, made my way up to the lockside and then wondered what on earth I was supposed to do! After many years and locks later I am amazed at my stupidity but I clearly remember wondering: which end? which side?

'Lift the paddle nearest you,' called Daphne as I hesitated. Worse still, from under the bridge ahead I could see the bows of another pair of boats travelling south.

'Boats coming,' I called waving my arms and pointing.

'Draw the lock,' she insisted. 'Quick.'

I fitted on the windlass and began to turn so that the water level in the lock began to sink more quickly. But those paddles! I heaved and strained to lift the first, and by the time I crossed over the intimidating height of those gates to flex my muscles on the second paddle the lock was almost empty. As I pulled at the gate to get it open, a boy of about ten or twelve – difficult to tell with boatboys – appeared on the other side.

'Saw you coming,' he called. 'S'alright – me dad's holding back.' For a boatboy he was almost garrulous; usually we couldn't get a word from them. He was one of the many Gardner boys who had become friendly with Kit and more familiar with this new breed of boatwomen.

'Trainees, ain't you?' he grinned as he opened the other gate with an easy grace. 'Let her swing. Don't need to shove so,' and indeed the gate began to swing open with such a force that I was always almost knocked backwards.

'You with Miss French? Kitty's up to the Arm.'

'Which arm?' I called as Daphne brought the boats into the chamber.

'Arm-end,' he called as we closed the gates. 'Northampton.'

I struggled with the winding gear on my side of the lock; I had to take a step onto a ledge of the gate and lean with all my strength on the windlass with each turn. Even the boy grunted as he turned.

'Only draw half,' he said. 'Don't want to swamp the boats.'

I saw that his boats were now idling at a safe distance from the lock. I asked him his name. He told me that it was Dave and that locks were ready for us as far as Stockers. When the lock was half full, Dave completed the turns on the paddle so that the water gushed through the open sluice, quickly filling the deep chamber. I had done the same on my side and sat on the balance beam to recover. In no time the lock was ready, the gates were opened and Daphne was taking the motor ahead. 'Get on board,' she called. 'Ten minutes to Widewater.'

All the locks had names: there was Black Jack, Copper Mill, Springwell, Stockers, Batch, Ricky and so on – all the way to Tyseley. There were to be 154 of them round to Fazeley in Birmingham, some of them spaced out and others in flights – Hatton had twenty-one. It took a few trips before I could remember all of them and also the names of certain bridges and bends. There was then no written record of these names, although Kit had compiled a typewritten sheet for her own convenience and that of her trainees. Now, there is every sort of map, chart and guide to provide the waterways traveller with lock-by-lock details of distances, lock depths, hazards, pubs, shops, repair yards, museums, tunnels, places of historic and picturesque interest to be visited along the way, Ordnance Survey maps to show almost every twist and turn of the canals in relation to the whole network of roads, by-roads, lanes and footpaths with which our small island is criss-crossed. During those war years there was not a single guide to the routes that we followed, and maps were unobtainable, the possession of one to be hidden rather than used.

Before the explosion of car ownership, when the lives of most, other than the wealthy, were narrowly parochial, geographical knowledge was largely limited to textbook information, and for myself and most of the other trainees those early trips along the

Grand Union and the Oxford were real voyages of discovery. Names were related to amenities, so that Fenny Stratford – known as Fenney – meant that we could replenish our store of evaporated milk (a concession to boat travellers that we could buy as many as we could afford); 'top of Atherstone' signified a butcher sympathetic to our needs; Leighton was a kindly lady who offered us baths, while Birmingham to us meant Littlewoods-and-peanut-butter, fish and chips, baths and a cinema.

As we continued on that first trip to Tyseley, Peggy and I took it in turns to be initiated into the motor work and there was little time or energy for any talk except that which related directly to the business of working the boats. We passed the Gardners with waves and a repetition of the information given to us by Dave. The old couple – probably only middle-aged – were working the boats with their young son; two other boys were in the Army.

'Left the gates open. Heard you were coming up,' added the steerer. The boatpeople could pinpoint almost to the hour where most of the other pairs were located; it was as if the whole route was imprinted upon their minds, the movement of boats as clearly registered as the coloured markers on any operational map.

With much trepidation I took the Capricorn into my first lock, trying to remember all that I had been told and all that I had observed when Daphne was at the tiller. Not too fast but fast enough to give the butty sufficient way-on to get it over the entrance of an uphill lock; loose off the towing strap as the butty bows draw up to the motor counter and throw the strap over the for'ard deck of the butty; steer the motor towards the centre of the cill at the far end of the chamber, then give a quick burst astern with the tiller firmly held to prevent its swinging against the side of the lock; into neutral immediately as the boat brakes and the bows swing to lie alongside the near wall while the butty nudges its way past, its speed to be checked by Peggy who has jumped(?) off and taken a couple of turns around the stump; take out the tiller pin and put it in the ticket drawer for safety; remove the tiller; tie the sterns of the boats for extra safety and turn the gearwheel for a few revs to keep the boats well forward; increase the revs as the inrush of water sweeps them back against the lower gates where the back fenders (tipcats) could get wedged under one of the crossbeams on the gates; as the beams of the rear gates are cleared and the lock is filled, into neutral again so that the boats drift back to enable the top gates to be opened. The stages raced through my mind as I concentrated fiercely on each and every move. My mouth was dry and my legs were rigid as we reached the top. Daphne signified approval from the bank, where she had been on the alert for any possible mishap. It was only later, when I was helping instruct the newcomers, that I could appreciate how much worse it was to be working the boats through the medium of a novice.

We tied up for dinner in Ricky (Rickmansworth), then pushed on through Casey (Cassiobury) bridge and the lovely stretch of parkland, round the vicious Lady Capel's bends where I was on the butty and had to 'row' with all my diminishing strength to edge the bows round the outside curves while Peggy, under Daphne's direction, put the motor hard ahead, steering into the bank so that the stern helped to pull the butty round. It was difficult enough to edge the motor round so that it did not become wedged across the sharp angle of the bend, and to get the butty clear as well without having to shaft the bows away from the bank was always a relief with loaded boats.

Daphne wanted to reach Fishery tie-up by Hemel Hempstead as she had heard that other trainees were likely to be there for the night; so we pushed on past Langley and Apsley mills until, finally, when we thought we could not face another lock, Daphne said we had arrived. No sign of any other boats!

We were eating supper when we heard the familiar thump of another National. It was dark and Daphne left us to give the new arrivals help with the lock.

'Hello there, Madge,' we heard her call and then the sounds of voices, the paddles on the winding gear and the rush of water below us. I opened the door a crack and looked out but could only see shapes as they moved around the lock. I retreated back into the cabin. I was much too tired to make any effort to join the new arrivals. Peggy too was slumped heavily against the bulkhead, her legs stretched out along the side-bed. I began the thankless job of clearing up after the meal while she sat there dozing.

It was Kay, Madge and Averil on Alcor and Alphons, said Daphne on her return. They had all arranged to meet for a drink in the pub later on. Peggy revived at the thought, saying that she could bloody well do with a bloody good drink. I said I was too tired. The thought of a hot, stuffy bar, the smell of drink and the effort to talk and listen through the noise held no attraction. I only wanted to stretch out my weary limbs in the comforting warmth of my bed and, in fact, I had no recollection of their return later that evening. Sleep was profound and dreamless.

The other crew had left in the morning before we emerged. They had coal for Glaxo and were hoping to get there early as Kay was off to meet a friend in London.

It was another locking day for us up through Berker (Berkhampstead), Dudswell and Cowroast to the Tring summit where we had a welcome rest before starting on the downhill locks at Marsworth, two and then a flight of seven.

I was on the motor for the first lock and took it too fast so that I crashed the gates at the far end, sending cascades of water spilling over the top. Then the butty came charging along in the deep water and hit the motor stern, which sent it crashing the gates again. Frantically I wound the gearwheel into reverse but it was too late to save the crashes. Peggy had been unable to negotiate the checking strap from the butty around the stump and was shouting at me for having taken the boats in too bloody fast and what the bloody hell did I think I was doing. Daphne muttered a hope that no one had heard the crashes. I shouted back that Daphne could take the motor herself and stalked off down to the next lock. It was empty, so I closed the bottom gates, drew a paddle and left the lock to fill while I continued on down the towpath. There was a fair stretch to the next locks but I didn't care. I wanted to be away from the blasted boats and from the ignominy of being shouted at. The other two could work the boats on their own. Nerves and tempers frayed by tiredness reduced most of us to levels of which we were later ashamed; luckily we also laughed at our mishaps when we relaxed over supper or, as on this evening, over pints in the Red Lion. As I mellowed I apologized for my churlish behaviour. Daphne said she wasn't surprised; others had been worse. We were both very tired, and it should be easier the next day when we would tie up in Leighton and possibly go to the cinema.

Peggy was very silent, too tired to complain, and the next morning she said she felt too ill to get up. She managed to eat a large bowl of porridge which Daphne took over to her. 'Just tired, I think,' said Daphne. 'Think we can manage?'

Confidence and optimism were renewed after nine hours of cataleptic sleep, and I nodded cheerfully, offering to take the motor. I took the boats into the next four locks with never a hitch; just the right angle and just the right speed. Daphne then took over so that I could make myself a mug of cocoa; we were always ready for elevenses by ten o'clock! We worked well together and I found the work easier without having to think always of a third person. However, by the time we reached Leighton, tiredness again was beginning to overtake me and I felt I could never wind another paddle. We shopped from Faulkners on the bridge and when we returned Peggy had surfaced. She had lit the fire and made us all some soup. We warmed to such magnanimity!

I revived with the hot soup and the remains of a rice pudding. It was still early afternoon and the hours ahead stretched emptily and without purpose. The itch to be travelling already was stirring in the blood. Then Daphne suggested that we might like to go on as far as Fenney; it was an easy run, with only the Leighton lock and the three at Stoke Hammond. At Fenney we could stock up with our tins of milk – our store under the side-bed had dwindled visibly – and there was a canalside pub. I volunteered to make another start on the oranges which had been neglected during the past days of almost continuous locking.

So on we went to tie up at the shallow lock at Fenney. It seemed an unnecessary sort of a lock, with only the drop of a few inches, and there was neither a gauging nor a toll office – just the pub. Daphne explained that the difference in the levels occurred where the two ends of the canal met when it was dug by the gangs of navvies, one team working from the north and the other from the south – pretty good judgement!*

We bought in our stock of evaporated milk which would enrich our mugs of cocoa and be used as cream on porridge and puddings and in a dozen different imaginative recipes to supplement our meagre diet. We treated ourselves to rum that evening, which sent a temporary sparkle through our tired muscles. No other boats were tied there and we had passed only four pairs travelling south since we had left Bull's Bridge. The landlord told us that most of the boats were going up empty to the coalfields as so many were fed up with waiting for orders at the docks. A pair

*See page 78.

of 'ours' had gone through a couple of days back but they had stopped only for milk and bread; he thought it was Margery. The talk between Daphne and the landlord continued intermittently – all about the boats and the crews, so that Peggy and I drank in lethargic silence.

Another day. Another right-angled bend, followed by a five-hour pound (a stretch with no locks). Daphne said we would take turns at steering the motor and that the one on the butty could cut up oranges while she steered! We would also use the snubber. This was a seventy-foot length of soft sisal rope which uncoiled lazily from the front deck of the butty where Daphne had coiled it in readiness. She remained stoically perched on the motor gunwale ready for any possible emergency. The weather held fair – no rain, for which we were thankful. The butty was so much easier to steer on the long length and it was peaceful with the thump of the engine far removed. After Cosgrove, as I leaned over the solid curve of the tiller, I saw mushrooms in a field alongside the canal and shouted to those ahead. I waved my arms and pointed to the bank. Daphne thought that something was amiss and throttled down. 'Mushrooms,' I shouted, expecting her to stop. We would fry them that evening with the spam we had bought at Fenney and my mouth watered at the thought. 'Mushrooms,' I shouted again and signalled that we might gather some. Daphne looked at the field, shrugged, shook her head and throttled up again.

'Too difficult to stop with loaded boats,' she explained later. 'Too much mud and even the shore plank would not have reached.'

Many, many years later, when my daughter Helen and I were travelling that way on the Alphons, we passed the same place. It was again early autumn, there were still mushrooms growing there and in the mist of an early morning Helen and I filled our plastic bags with them.

Meanwhile there were the oranges which I continued to deal with on the cabin top as I gave the occasional shove on the butty tiller to keep the boat on course. At Stoke Bruerne there were more locks and a surly lock-keeper who refused to help us, but at the top there was a welcome respite in yet another of the old pubs, the Boat, which still is a mecca for boat talk and visits to the canalside museum. The next morning came Blisworth tunnel, headlights, a short towing strap and forty minutes of chugging our route towards the pinpoint of light which grew slowly into the semicircle from which we emerged blinking into the misty light of a September morning. Peggy and I were on the butty for mutual support during that first incursion into the underworld but I was totally fascinated by the strangeness of our journey through this underground channel. In the arc of light from the headlamp I could see that the bricked walls were hung with occasional patches of orange fungi despite the apparent dryness of the brickwork. I was content to steer and stare while Peggy brewed up down in the cabin. There was a shaft of light ahead and, as I gazed upwards towards this funnel in the roof, I was deluged by a spatter of water draining through from the fields under which we were burrowing. It was the first of the vent holes which we soon learned to dodge as we passed underneath.

The entries in my journal almost ceased until there is a brief entry for 11 September at Leamington: *Locks. Hundreds of them. Bends. Narrow bridge'oles. Mud. Passing boats. Every conceivable danger and difficulty has been met with during the past week. No one could possibly imagine all the troubles and trials of a boatman's life. For twelve solid hours from 7 a.m.'* I read with surprise of such an early start, as Daphne reckoned to break us in gently for our first trip! We must have been held up with 'dangers and difficulties' and needed to make up the time. No trip was ever as arduous as that first one, not even the memorable trip the following January when we were ice-bound for over a week at the Blue Lias.

We came to Hatton. Taking a breasted pair of loaded boats up through those twenty-one locks for the first time was – and still must be – a make-or-break experience. The staircase stretched upwards and ahead between the strange white posts of the paddle gear like a Jacob's ladder leading to some unknown and uncharted territory. Peggy was to lockwheel and I was to take the motor, and I felt nervous as hell at the thought of steering those heavily laden coffins into the narrow confines of the locks. Daphne stood in the well of the butty to continue her instructions and to be ready for stepping off as the stern drew level with the stone coping. I had grown confident with taking the motor through the downhill locks back at Stoke Hammond and Braunston and the well-spaced ones on the Itchington stretch but these were different, formidable in the continuous continuity of their ascent. At the sight of them all my diffidence and nervous apprehension returned. As we approached the first lock, I was too tentative in my use of the engine and Daphne just managed to grab the tiller and to pull it hard over so that, instead of hitting the coping, the boats grazed and grated their way into the lock without too much damage.

'Astern,' called Daphne as she stepped off. 'Now slightly ahead so that the water doesn't rush the boats back against the gates.' Despite all the uphill locks we had negotiated already, my mind seemed to be a blank and I was glad of the repeated instructions.

'Often happens,' consoled Daphne later on.

By this time I was sweating freely and gladly would have changed places with Peggy on that endless round of lockwheeling. On a subsequent trip I did in fact lockwheel up Hatton while another novice endured the ordeal of being in charge of the boats. It was a dull November day, with rain and mist greasing the slime on the lock gates and gradually soaking through my boots and old mac. Twenty-one locks and all against us! At the top I collapsed on the ground, wet, hungry, exhausted and wretched. It was my birthday; no one cared!

Entrances to many of the locks had their own peculiarities and irregularities; no two seemed to be the same. The gate of one would begin to swing closed as the boats approached. 'Keep going,' shouted Daphne as I throttled down to give her time to open it again so that I would not crash into it; as unpredictably it began to close and swing back into position as the boats came nearer, and a gentle nudge from the motor tucked it away for the last few inches. At the entrance to another a fierce sluice of water volleyed the bows away from the line of entrance to the lock. 'Hard over,' shouted Daphne, rowing with an arm to enforce urgency of response. It took a steady nerve to keep the engine at full throttle until the boats were safely over the cill and then to wind the gearwheel into hard astern while the tiller was held in the small of a back to keep it from swinging.

'Tiller off,' shouted Daphne from way above me as I strove to find the neutral position on the gearwheel. I wrenched out the tiller pin and pulled off the heavy brass tiller to lay it along the cabin top. 'How many more?' I groaned to myself. I had lost all count.

'Ahead now,' Daphne's voice penetrated my state of near-catalepsy so that I responded to her orders with the automatic reflex of a puppet.

'You did fine.' The words halted me in my decision to step off and refuse to take the responsibility of the boats through another lock. By the time we reached the top I was taking the boats without further instructions from Daphne – a make-or-break situation! It took us five hours to work up through the flight. On working boats we did it in half the time! I began to develop a preference for downhill locks, a preference I still maintain, although it now seems so easy to work with a single powered boat by comparison with a loaded pair.

We had passed the BWB workshops and at the top we met with George the fitter, who was always a great friend and ally to all the trainees in our many and varied vicissitudes.

'Saw you coming up,' he said cheerfully. 'I've been oiling the gates specially for your friend here.'

Peggy was stretched out on the ground and I could but sympathize.

'Bloody gates. Bloody paddles. Bloody oil didn't make any difference,' she muttered.

Relations between Peggy and myself were still strained and finally were ruptured one evening as we were nearing Tyseley. We had struggled up Hatton 21 and were tying up at the top of Knowle, yet another flight of five locks all with very heavy gates and stiff winding gear. I was tying the for'ard line when she came breezing up.

'Come for a drink tonight,' she said. 'Just you and me. Not Daph. Reckon we've earned a good booze-up.'

I had no excuse ready except that I had no wish to go to the pub for a booze-up. My sham attempts at mateyness became all too apparent. I forget her response except that she went on her own and returned much later with a noisy escort. The boats were breasted up with the motor on the outside in the deeper water; if they had been singled out, there would have been no difficulty for Peggy and her escort to have reached her cabin. As it was, they stood on the towpath outside our cabin, and Peggy's comments were obviously meant for our ears. 'Bloody stuck-up – both of them . . . Sodding work and no bloody play . . .'

We were both in bed and lay there, left in no doubt of her

opinion of us. The man who had been 'singing' his own version of 'Run, rabbit, run' seemed otherwise to be inarticulate. Daphne told me to put on the light and was prepared to go out if necessary. There followed a period of silence and we thought they had gone off down the towpath. Then, 'Bugger off,' we heard Peggy say. Gone too far, I thought, but then we heard her gagging.

'Not over the boat,' muttered Daphne.

The retching stopped and the boat lurched as she crawled into the butty well-deck.

'Goodnight,' called Daphne, urbane as ever. There was no reply as we heard her clamber over into the motor cabin. Luckily there was no ominous splash which we half expected. The man must have cleared off, as we heard nothing more from him.

The next morning Daphne made no reference to the previous evening except to ask her if she felt strong enough to steer the butty. Daphne took over a bucket of the oranges to cut up while she stood on the gunwale of the motor and I steered.

At Tyseley, Peggy told Daphne that she'd be leaving; the boats weren't for her. I felt both relieved and guilty. Daphne said that it was a question of temperament. She would telephone Miss Minn to see if there was anyone waiting to join the boats who could meet us in Coventry. She decided we would take the empty boats breasted up back through Norton Junction and then northwards to Coventry. She said it would be easier than going two-handed round the Lower Road, where there were single locks. I was disappointed at not continuing this voyage of discovery; nothing could be worse than Knowle and Hatton all over again. I was yet to learn!

We were lucky and met with the pairs which had been tied with us back in the dock. Two of the pairs were carrying crates of tinned meat. Daphne had a fair stock of good burning coal stored in the bunker, and buckets were soon filled and passed across in exchange for several tins from a crate which had broken open during the loading.

'Good to have something in store when we can't get our emergency rations,' grinned Daphne.

'Getting harder an' all,' said one of the boatmen. 'Got to look after our own or we'd starve for all they care.'

Lucky too that we met with one pair coming up the Knowle

locks and the other two pairs working up Hatton so that all the locks were ready for us. There was no wind, and with the empty boats tied together we were down the twenty-one in just three hours. Again I began to enjoy my growing skill with managing the boats and the increasing ease with which I could wind the paddles and move the gates. I had changed plimsolls for an old, tough pair of walking shoes and found them far more suitable for digging in heels to move the heavy gates. I make a further note in my diary to follow Ben's advice and scour the Limehouse back-streets for boots the next time we were down that way.

At the bottom of Hatton we singled out the boats with the butty pulled up close to the motor with short, crossed straps. Between the well-spaced Itchington locks we were able to take turns off and to relax in the warmth of the butty cabin – while we boiled up yet more pans of marmalade! In no time we were back at Norton Junction north of Braunston, where the top Oxford branches off from the main line to lead through to Hawkesbury and the coalfields. At the turn was a delightful cottage which housed the headquarters of the Salvation Army, whose members did such valuable work among the boatpeople.

Footnote to page 72: In fact, the truth as told by Alan Faulkner in his *Grand Junction Canal* is more prosaic. Between Fenny and Wolverton, the canal leaked extensively, the worst length being the 2 miles north of Fennny where it proved impossible to maintain a sufficient depth of water for loaded boats. As a temporary measure, a lock was built at Fenny in 1802 and the pound to Wolverton was lowered by about a foot. Since then, no-one has risked the expense and disruption which its removal would occasion.

4. Jo

At Hawkesbury stop Daphne went to the office and returned
with orders to load at Longford. It was 'just around the corner',
and an easy loading place. Daphne said we would take the boats
round and then she'd take a bus into Coventry to meet the new
recruit. Miss Minn had phoned Mr Vieter in the office to give him
the details but all he knew was the time of the train when she
would arrive and that her name was Jo and that they were to meet
in the ladies' room at the station.

There was yet another of those tricky right-angled bends under
a bridge where we would turn left for loading and, while Daphne
was away in the office, I watched a loaded pair negotiate the bend
on their return trip southwards. As the motor nosed slowly
through the gap, a girl jumped off the for'ard deck with a line.
Now I could see the reason for an iron bollard positioned on the
coping under the bridge. She took a turn round it with the rope
and, as the length of the boat eased into the boat's length of water
in the small basin ahead, she gradually eased the line in its turn
around the bollard so that it pulled the bows of the motor around
the bend. In the narrowness of the passage under the bridge it
was not possible for the steerer to row the length of the boat
around the angle but, with the pull on the bows, it was safely
round without getting jammed against the opposite bank. The

butty followed at a discreet distance on its length of towing line and was manœuvred around by the judicious use of the motor. I watched, fascinated by the expertise, knowing that soon I would be responsible for negotiating a pair of loaded boats back through the awkwardness of the turn.

Taking the empty boats through on a short strap was relatively easy, and soon we were tied up by the gritty bank of the loading length. There was a slight wind, and coal dust filled the air. As Daphne left for Coventry, she cautioned me to keep the hatch pulled over and the cabin doors closed as the dust would get in everywhere.

While she was gone, I washed my hair again and tied it up in a scarf. Despite the closed doors the coal dust *was* everywhere. The taste of it was in my mouth, and it layered the shelves and surfaces. Coaling up always left everything and everyone grimed and grey and gritty despite all our precautions to exclude the all-pervading dust from the cabins and our clothes. We donned button-through overalls, tied them at wrists and ankles, bound up our hair in scarves and kept the cabin doors sealed as tightly as possible by bolting them and pulling the hatch cover over the top during the two hours when the coal was plummeted down the chutes into the holds. As the chutes were fixed structures, we had to move the boats along into position by standing on the pile of coal deposited in the hold and pull on the girders of the chute moving the boat along ready to receive the next avalanche. When the boats had received their loads of twenty and twenty-five tons apiece, we roughly levelled out the heaped piles with shovels and then pulled the boats back to the mooring rings so that the next pair could move into the loading place. We had already winded (turned) the boats when they were empty, and they were now ready for the return trip.

I had plenty to fill my thoughts as I squeezed and cut up yet more of the diminishing pile of oranges. I wondered what the newcomer would be like and if she would stay and how we would get on together. I felt a guilt squirm as I thought of the ambivalence of my relationship with Peggy. I had tried to find some level of rapport between us, not satisfied until I had succeeded. Then, as she had warmed to me, I had withdrawn and she had seen me for the phoney that I was. I still sigh at the memory of unresolved problems incurred by the paradox of the need to be involved with others and the need to be detached. I thought – and wrote! – that I would be more wary of the newcomer, keep my distance, curb my interest in personal background, restrict conversation to the boats and the work we were doing. Little did I know that such intentions were as chaff before the wind with the arrival of Jo.

My first impression of Jo was that of a slight, curly-haired young woman with a deep, throaty voice. We met over the interminable mugs of watered-down tea, both wary and both reticent while Daphne eased the meeting with her account of the trip into Coventry. She had been shocked by the extent of bomb damage to the city.

That evening, after we had been loaded, we negotiated the turn through the bridge. Jo was instructed to ease the bows of the motor around with a line to the checking stump. She seemed to understand immediately what was required; she was a 'natural', I thought enviously. Daphne and Jo went off to the Greyhound for drinks but I chose to remain behind – a vain effort to initiate the defensive stratagem I had decided to adopt with the new recruit. Also I really disliked the cold beer with its bitter taste, and I was too broke to afford anything better.

'She's going to be good,' said Daphne later, when they returned. 'Bit of a show-off – says she's worked on a coaster.'

'Hope you're right,' I said tetchily, barely disguising the scepticism I felt about such information.

The next morning Jo was up, had lit the fire in her cabin and was polishing the brass porthole by the time we emerged.

'Thought you said we'd be off to an early start,' she said. It was still only eight and Daphne said we'd be ready in half an hour.

'All right if I try a hand at steering Capricorn, Skipper?' the new recruit asked breezily as we stood on the bank ready to get the engine going and to untie the mooring ropes. Daphne welcomed such a positive approach and agreed readily. I felt resentment rising and made for the engine-room. It was Jo who helped Daphne to swing the flywheel while I pushed over the compression lever. She made the turning of the handle so effortlessly – she could have done it on her own, I thought.

The trip progressed smoothly and easily. Jo's steering was faultless and Daphne relaxed from her vigilant stance on the gunwale to perch on the cabin roof. The long stretches of the top

Oxford were peaceful and idyllic on another of those quiet autumn days. At the end of the seventy-foot length of snubber the noise from the engine was barely audible, and I leaned on the great wooden tiller to watch the moorhens, the small flotillas of ducks and the mottled decadence of the hedgerows as we passed. The cows looked up dolefully and impassively and I began to sing again!

The scene is imprinted indelibly upon my memory, and each time I have passed that way in later years I find myself humming the old tunes of Clementine, the Wraggle-Taggle gipsies and Upidee with which I then regaled the countryside in full voice!

At Hillmorton locks we tied up for a quick meal and I thought we might have had a change-over and that Jo would take a turn on the butty, but Daphne said we should continue as before as far as Braunston. The Braunston locks were ready, and Daphne signalled that we'd keep going. She took over the motor while Jo went ashore to open the bottom gates of the first lock. Feeling agreeable and relaxed after the long stretches of solitude, I agreed to continue with the butty work. We seemed to fly up the locks in record time with never a hitch or a misjudgement. Jo seemed to know by instinct the most efficient way of working the gates and the paddles with barely a word of instruction from Daphne. She wound up the paddles with an ease which I envied; I began to think she had worked on a coaster after all.

'Mind if I stay on the motor?' she asked at the top. 'Just getting the hang of it.'

'There's the tunnel' – I thought perhaps to intimidate her.

'Great. A change from just trekking along,' she breezed.

Daphne was checking the headlights and asked me if I would mind staying on the butty as Jo was so keen to take the motor through the tunnel. I shrugged, slightly annoyed yet secretly relieved that the ordeal of taking the motor through one of the long tunnels would be deferred.

'Keep the tiller on the inside width of the boat or it could jam against the wall,' she advised. 'Flick the light if you're in trouble.'

We chugged our way through the darkness with no difficulty and met with only one pair coming north. I had a moment's panic as the bows of the Cleopatra were pulled out by the bow wave from the oncoming motor but with a few frantic rows I was able to straighten up before the two butties slid past each other. There were shouts and laughs as we exchanged greetings in the anonymity of that dark, underground passageway.

Daphne decided we should tie up for the night at Stowe Hill wharf, and that evening, after a very late tea and a wash, we all three went to the Globe (now the Narrow Boat) for drinks. Daphne was tired and began to nod in the warmth of the small bar. Jo soon tired of my unresponsive comments to her blustering talk and took herself off to impress the barman with her talk of the boats, the state of the locks and her own feats of strength and competence. I left them and walked along the road to lean over the bridge and admire the slim shapes of the boats below.

I feigned sleep when they returned. I felt an irrational irritation with them both. 'Two's company . . .' I thought as they came aboard, 'and I'm the odd one out . . .'

The next morning over an early breakfast Daphne said that I should take the motor and she would initiate Jo into the butty work. Jo had other ideas! She asked for details of the day's work ahead and was told, 'Two-and-a-half-hour pound, another long tunnel and then seven downhill locks at Stoke.' She would take the motor as far as Stoke and then take the butty down the locks, when I could take the motor. Daphne hesitated but found Jo's enthusiasm too hard to resist. She looked at me and I shrugged my indifference. It was Daphne's decision. I was still only a newcomer who had not even completed my first round trip. Jo had the knack of taking over and settling indecisions by her own forthright deliberations, taken with a breeze of confidence. I remember feeling bitchy about Daphne's acquiescence to Jo's preference for the motor. I enjoyed the privacy of being left alone on the butty where I could warm my feet by the fire, make myself a pot of tea as I steered and ruminate over the strangeness of this nomadic existence, but at the same time I resented Jo's dominance and Daphne's easy compliance with her demands.

So Jo had her way and took Capricorn past the old coal wharf, past the blackberry bushes which threw their laden branches out over the Cut so temptingly just out of reach. There are still bushes of wild sloes and crab apples along that stretch where I now stop the Alphons at leisure to gather that wild profusion of 'food for free'. But then we just kept going through the bridge'oles and the twists and turns of that lovely stretch of the Grand Union. It was raining as we came to Blisworth tunnel, and it was pleasant to enter the womb-like shelter under the hills. I was ready for the occasional downpours from the round air-vents in the roof, pulled over the hatch cover and dived for shelter as the water spattered its way along the cabin roof towards me.

At the top of Stoke I grudgingly took over the motor while Daphne and Jo stood talking to the lock-keeper.

'We'll go down singled out for practice,' said Daphne. 'Sid says the locks are all ready for us,' and I remembered that we had passed two – or was it three? – pairs on the pound down from Stowe. 'We'll breast up for the middle three.'

I made a real mess of those first two locks, took them too fast for downhill locks where there was a good depth of water, crashed the gates and gave the butty too much speed so that even Jo found it difficult to check the onward rush into the lock.

'Take it easy. Much slower . . . much slower,' shouted Daphne after near disaster in the second lock. Her fault, all her fault, I thought viciously; what does she expect when I haven't been on the motor for days? Sid came over from the side-pond into which he had been emptying half a lockful of water. He was a different lock-keeper from the churlish one we had met on the way up.

'New, aren't you?' he said grinning at me. 'Take it easy like Miss French says. There's no rush and you do better taking it slow. Downhill locks any road . . . plenty of water on this stretch. Different now when you come to Maffas.'

The rain trickled down the neck of my old gaberdine mac and dripped into my tough walking shoes. I could have howled with rage and mortification. Why had I come on these blasted boats anyway?

He turned back to lower the paddle on the side-pond as I gulped back tears of aggravation at my incompetence. Then I felt my face and mind set into the mask of cussedness which has often held the reins over the more diffident side of my nature. I felt coldly capable. I'd show them; especially I'd show that over-confident Jo that I was as good as she.

We tied up at the bottom of the locks for a late dinner.

'You took those locks really well,' said Daphne as she dished out the stew.

'After the first two,' I muttered, 'but of course I had to get used to taking the motor again.'

'Sorry,' said Daphne. 'The trouble is she's so good. I don't like to discourage her.'

I knew what she meant; we needed someone to stay. Working boats were being laid up for lack of crews and already, on my first trip, we had lost both Mary and Peggy.

'It's all right,' I replied. 'I don't really mind. I just feel such a fool when I mess things up.'

'I'll have to be tougher with her. But it's difficult.'

I knew and she knew that she would have to be very tough indeed. She hadn't a hope!

Jo came over to spoon out the rest of the stew from the saucepan. It was warm and cosy there in the cabin with the rain continuing its deluge outside.

There came a rap on the cabin side and we heard Sid's voice saying that one of us had left a windlass lying on the beam of the gate. It was Jo's windlass. I felt smugly gratified!

'What comes next skipper?' she asked breezily when Sid had returned back up the locks.

'Long straight stretch to Fenney, where we'll tie up,' said Daphne.

'I'll stay on the motor then,' said Jo casually yet assertively. 'You have a turn tomorrow, Meg,' she added as I glared my resentment at her presumption. I resented too her abbreviation of my name; I had been Meg to someone now dead, and her use of the name was an intrusion into a private grief which had barely healed.

'My name is Margaret,' I said coldly, 'and I prefer to be called that.'

'Fine by me, Mar-gar-et,' she mocked me, 'and mine is Jo-se-phine.'

'Time to get going,' interrupted Daphne. 'Come on, Jo, and help me start the engine.'

I cleared up as they left, deciding that I would not get rattled by Jo. The thought of another four or five weeks of working together would be tolerable only if I could learn to accept her assertive attitude. She *was* good, I had to admit. I wondered if there would be another recruit waiting for us at the depot and if that would ease or aggravate the situation.

'You all right on your own?' Daphne asked as the boats came alongside at the shallow – and then isolated – Cosgrove lock.

'I'm fine,' I replied with overmuch enthusiasm as she dived into the cabin for warmth, cocoa and bucket. Jo had taken the motor ahead and was idling as she waited for Daphne to rejoin her. Reluctantly Daphne emerged.

'Freezing standing there on the motor,' she said. 'I was hoping for a turn on the butty – but you know Jo. She's too good to discourage.' Daphne sounded hesitant, as if she was about to add something else, but Jo had backed Capricorn to the lock gate for Daphne to get aboard.

'Ready, Skipper?' she called. Daphne turned up her coat collar and reluctantly rejoined Jo on the motor. A small glow of sadistic satisfaction offset feelings of rancour as I watched her cup hands around the warmth of the chimney. What was so special about Jo anyway?

The rain began to ease as the boats slowly made their way down to Fenney. Daphne's attention seemed to be focused more on what Jo was saying than on the way ahead and I wondered idly what the tale could be. Meanwhile I continued to enjoy the comforts of the butty, made myself a thick sandwich and dried off shoes and trousers by the fire as I steered from the shelter of the hatchway with the cabin doors closed and latched behind me.

We had met with no other boats and there were none at Fenney where we tied up, filled the water cans, washed and made a meal. 'More sardines!' I noted in my diary.

Later, the three of us went off to the bar/shop to buy our tins of milk and whatever other provisions the shop could offer. I left Jo and Daphne to go for a short walk and to phone a friend in London to say I hoped to be around at the end of the week. When I returned to the boats, I could hear Jo in the cabin of the Cleopatra and I almost turned back into the pub. But money was short and it was cold and I was tired. I entered noisily. Jo was lying along the side-bed with her head on Daphne's lap. I felt embarrassed; Daphne looked embarrassed, but Jo remained imperturbable and stayed where she was.

'Had a good walk, Mar-gar-et?' she asked.

I ignored her, stepped over to the back end of the cabin and let down the bed flap. 'I'm tired,' I said briefly trying to ignore them.

'Time to go now, Jo,' said Daphne as I began to strip off. To my surprise she went without the expected bluster.

'She has problems,' offered Daphne by way of explanation.

'So have we all. I don't want to know,' I replied churlishly, crawled into bed and turned my back to the hostility in the cabin. Was Jo a lesbian? Were they both lesbians? I wondered as I drifted into sleep.

We continued our way southwards and I was allowed (by Jo!) to take the motor up through Stoke Hammond three and along to Leighton, where we tied up for shopping and dinner. Daphne and I were coldly polite to each other while Jo buzzed and chattered between us like a bee-busy social worker. We worked up the Marsworth flight, taking it in turns on the motor and the butty while Daphne went ahead to open gates and to empty the locks where necessary. We said little or nothing to each other and I guessed that Daphne had told Jo I should take my turn on the motor.

We tied for the night at Cowroast on the summit and again we were joined in the butty cabin by Jo, who took up her position along the side-bed with her head on Daphne's lap. She began to tell us that she was a writer and that she had come on the boats to collect material for her new book. I didn't want to hear and left the cabin to walk along to the pub. I didn't want a drink and I didn't want to return to the boats. I found a phone but my friends in London all seemed to be out. How could I have been so foolhardy and stupid to have chucked my job and left the warm comfort of my room in Chelsea? – wishfully forgetting that I might well have been adrift in some other remote area of an evacuation campaign. I think that, had we been near a railway station, I would have taken a train straight back to London and redressed my sideways step onto the canals. There was little else to do but to walk and when, eventually, I returned to the boats, lights were out in both cabins and Daphne was asleep.

There followed two hard days of locking and we were all too tired for much personal chat. Each evening Jo came into the cabin and dominated both of us. I was too tired to go out and somehow Jo took over and no kind of rebuff seemed possible. I resented her familiarity while at the same time I envied her lack of inhibition.

We offloaded our cargo of coal at the Heinz factory near Greenford, a favourite destination with all boatpeople as we were allowed to take free meals in the canteen, a real bonus for the ever-hungry trainees. Then we were off to the docks again for yet another consignment of those iron pilings. We had a spare day as we waited for the dockers to come and plummet the bundles of rusty iron rods into the holds of our diminutive boats. During the few hours of spare time Daphne and I made our way up the iron-runged ladder set into the wall and headed for the shops in Commercial Road. Jo had offered to stay behind to keep an eye on the boats and I was glad to be free of her and to enjoy the easy camaraderie which already existed between Daphne and myself despite all the irritations and intrusions. 'Off the boats' was the password for exit and entry through the lock gates and then we were back into the mainstream of living. There were the familiar red buses hustling up and down and people hurrying along the pavements; there was the odd assortment of clothes shops, Chinese restaurants, where customers were inspected from behind bead curtains, junkshops, scrapyards and blankly mysterious walls and alleyways. We never dared to brave the questionable reputation of Commercial Road after dark; the narrow lane leading from the dock gateway was black and unlit in those days, when air raids were becoming frequent and fearful. Daphne pointed out 'The Prospect of Whitby', a favourite rendezvous for boatpeople of every kind, where we always found a welcome, even if that welcome was often rather too boisterous for comfort!

The shop we were heading for was inconspicuous in a street of similar frontages, and the interior was dark, with festoons of overalls and trousers blotting out the daylight from window and doorway. On that first visit I bought longjohns and sailors' vests, a pair of sailors' trousers with a front flap and a strong, sturdy pair of men's boots – all without coupons. We were never allocated any of the extra clothing coupons, and no uniforms were issued. The Land Army women looked resplendent in their green and buff 'going out' uniforms but it was their working overalls and boots, warm underwear and socks that we coveted so often. We were too small a group to be recognized for such extras as a few clothing coupons or a few extra ounces of cheese or meat. There were times when we felt very ill-treated, when we compared our lot with that of friends in the Services and the Land Army, although it is significant that none of us chose to desert the canals for the land despite rumours of pigs and butter, milk and eggs on the black market.

Back on the boats I pulled on one of the rough, long-sleeved vests over my own flimsy inadequacy, and a pair of the longjohns under my ski-ing trousers; the serge trousers I would reserve for the really cold days. At last I felt warm and comfortable in clothes properly suited to life on working boats. On the following trip I bought dungarees and a rough kind of reefer jacket. I could have done with a good oilskin but couldn't afford the luxury so that my old mac grew more grimy and rain-sodden through the ensuing weeks. I finally discarded it on a rubbishtip outside Fazeley after I had bought a short black oilskin and fisherman's helmet from a market stall.

5. Training Boats: Second Trip

On the return trip from the dock we were to meet Sandra at the Maida Vale stop, and she was there waiting for us, a small, indifferent-looking figure with a large, battered suitcase; I wondered where she would find space enough to stow it. She was thirty-ish and had been a secretary; so much Daphne had learned from Miss Minn at the Ministry. The precise nature of her past employment was never made more explicit even as she herself remained a closed, solitary figure devoid of past associations and background. I see her now as she stood there waiting for the boats, a rather pathetic figure with her battered brown suitcase, and wonder again whatever could have been the motive which drew her to step into a way of life so completely alien to all she had known.

Jo eyed her apprehensively, put on a great show of exuberant camaraderie and heaved up the suitcase with accompanying horseplay.

'Welcome aboard, shipmate,' she bawled, turning to wink at Daphne, whose more immediate concern was with the boats to ensure that they were tied free of the channel. It was a busy place, with boats waiting to have their cargoes gauged at the toll office nearby.

I went into the cabin to make tea and peanut-butter sandwiches, a gesture of welcome to the new recruit. Jo and Sandra, I thought. How? Not my concern.

She came over with Daphne for introduction and some preliminary instruction. Jo followed and perched herself on the step in the open hatchway.

'You'll soon get the hang of it all,' she assured the quiet person sitting by me and sipping the hot tea. Her hands, cupped around the mug were pale, unmuscular and with varnished nails. Under the navy raincoat she wore a fawn-coloured pullover and navy slacks; fawn-coloured lisle stockings ending in a pair of thin, flat-heeled shoes completed the outfit. The ropes would murder those soft hands and she'd feel every grit on the rough towpaths in those thin shoes. I looked smugly at my own square-toed boots in which my feet were now encased and thought of the inadequacy of my own tough walking shoes while the plimsolls were now just used as slippers. Perhaps there would be something more useful, more suitable, in the suitcase. There wasn't. Throughout the trip she wore the same clothes, and it was only later that we learned that neither she nor Jo even undressed for bed!

But Sandra persisted. There was a streak of determination behind those pale blue eyes which denied all her physical deficiencies as a potential boatwoman. We were marooned together for long hours on the butty; she endured my dictatorial instructions and my caustic comments on her general incompetence to cope with the daily chores of cooking and cleaning. Sadistically I made her clean the brasses, peel the potatoes, fill the water cans at the lock sides, fill the coal bucket, scrub the deck and cabin top, splice the ends of a new cotton line, make the cocoa and then go off to lockwheel while I leaned leisurely over the butty tiller. Jo and Daphne were still firmly rooted on the motor as we threaded our way up through the endless locks.

Then, at Albert's Two, Daphne said that either Sandra or I should take a turn at steering the motor. Jo said she'd lockwheel – anything rather than steer the butty. Sandra quietly but firmly refused; she said she was too scared and that she needed another day or two to get more used to the butty work. So I took over the motor on my own – not without trepidation – while Daphne took a well-earned 'rest' on the butty with Sandra. I was still resentful of the monopoly which Jo exercised over the proceedings, and screwed my resentment into a determination to prove my own efficiency in taking over the role of steerer. Jo soon tired of her own company on the towpath and at the third Winkwell lock said I should take my turn at lockwheeling. I refused and Daphne was forced to mediate. Sandra offered to go as we stood there glaring at each other.

'I'll go,' offered Sandra, 'so long as I can walk.' Riding a bicycle was another of her undeveloped skills.

Jo had won as usual except that I firmly refused to relinquish the tiller so that she perched herself on the gunwale while I steered. 'Thinks she's the trainer,' I thought, ignoring her and staring straight ahead.

'I'm a writer,' she began again, crashing through my hostility. I refused to answer and she went on to say that she wrote under another name and that I'd recognize it if she told me, that she was going to see her publisher when we got to Birmingham. She chattered on in that gravelly voice of hers, her talk punctuated with innuendos about her reputation, her achievements, her ambitions as a writer.

'Shut up,' I shouted at length. 'I need to concentrate.'

'Has Jo told you about her writing?' I asked Daphne that night in the minutes before sleep. Jo and Sandra had joined us for supper and had spent the evening by the warmth of our fire, Jo dozing in her favourite position. I had been glad of her silence for once and wondered what Sandra made of it all. She was further-ing her ability to splice under Daphne's watchful eye while I busied myself with writing up my diary. They had left reluctantly to the cold comfort of their cabin with the fire out.

'Oh yes,' Daphne replied in a whisper, 'and I don't believe a word of it.'

I was stunned – more to Daphne than I'd realized. I too had been sceptical of Jo's claims to fame but Daphne's downright rebuttal indicated a shrewdness of perception which belied the charm of her easy-going amiability.

'She's going to see her publisher in Birmingham,' I persisted, hoping for some more enlightenment on the enigmatic Jo.

'She has problems,' was all that Daphne would say. 'Good-night,' she said firmly.

It was to be an eventful trip, although we reached Tyseley without argument or confrontation. I think we were too tired most of the time to oppose Jo's obstinate preference for the motor. Grudgingly I was forced to acknowledge her competence and was resigned to stay on the butty with Sandra for most of the time. On the longer pounds between locks I made the most of my leisure, as Sandra preferred to steer and was disinclined to talk – a restful change from the garbled rantings of Jo each evening. The weather was kind – even warm – so that on the longer pounds I spent hours sitting on the bunker at the back end of the butty cabin splicing old ropes and fashioning a fender from odd pieces of rope salvaged from the Cut and from the towpath where mangled remains had been prodded out from the shafting by some boatman unlucky enough to have picked it up in the blades as he passed. Occasionally there were odd ends abandoned on the decks of the timber barges left unguarded for the night and we felt no qualms of conscience as we grabbed at any such loose ends left lying around. The supply of ropes, cotton lines, fenders and tipcats was minimal, and a boat with well-fashioned fenders, good lines and topstrings indicated a crew with sharp eyes and smart hands. There was a good supply of odd ends well hidden from other, light-fingered boatmen under the boards across the bunker and provided me with the perfect excuse to sit there in peace during the pounds beyond Blisworth and Braunston. The oranges, finally, had all been dealt with back in the dock.

I lockwheeled up Hatton and Knowle. Did I mind? asked Daphne, and irascibly I replied that it would make no difference if I did! I'd asked Sandra how she got on with Jo and she'd replied, 'All right,' and that they didn't see much of each other. They were just in the cabin to sleep, and Jo got up first to make the breakfast, which was mostly tea. They didn't bother to light the fire as the primus made some warmth in the mornings. Daphne or Jo sometimes lit the fire during the day – to keep their feet warm, she added.

At Tyseley Jo disappeared while Daphne and Sandra went off for baths and shopping. I volunteered to stay with the boats and to start on the work of preparing them for offloading. All I had to do was to untie the topstrings and roll up the sidecloths. The top planks would be lifted off and onto the bank when the others returned. I settled down to enjoy the peace.

'Boats ready for offloading?' called a voice.

Men, four of them, stood looking down into the contents

of the hold. Panic. What was I supposed to do? Where was Daphne?

'Miss French's boats aren't they?'

'She's gone into town. Not sure when she'll be back. Anything I should do?'

'That's all right, Miss. We'll take off the planks. You take it easy.'

Peace was shattered as the men heaved the iron rods ashore – the second time we had carried iron pilings north from the docks. It made me wonder at the economics of paying wages and for fuel to transport such cargoes through the countryside, but it was wartime and almost everything seemed to operate in mysterious and irrational ways – not for such as us to question! The boat lurched and jolted as the men heaved and grunted, two to each boat. I lay along the side-bed, resigned at the intrusion into my free time. Daphne would be pleased to see the empty boats on her return. It was impossible to read, even to make tea, as the men worked through the next hour or so. They finished just as Daphne and Sandra returned.

'Good,' said Daphne cheerfully. 'We can start tomorrow for Coventry. The Lower Road,' she added, making it sound like a threat.

Jo arrived later with a flourish and packets of fish and chips. We had just eaten supper but we welcomed the generous gesture and made more tea – or, rather, we added more hot water to the well-used leaves in the pot.

'Been to see George,' she breezed. 'My brother. In gaol.'

'Well now,' said Daphne unperturbed, 'how did you find him?'

'He's dreadfully ill – glandular fever. We're twins, and I knew something was wrong. I can feel all that happens to him and I knew that I had to go and see him.'

We gulped down the dramatics with the tea. Was it true? I asked about the publisher but Jo said there had been no time. George needed her and she had to go. Her look of innocent concern assailed my doubts. She looked tired and dirty. Where *had* she been? We held back the questions in an abortive attempt to deflect the torrent of melodrama which threatened to submerge us for the rest of the evening. Only Sandra swallowed the bait. 'Is he in hospital then?' she asked in a voice laced with sympathy, and Jo was launched into an extraordinary confusion

94

of loquacity ending in a vicious and semi-hysterical reviling of prisons, the law and authority in general. She and Peggy between them would have blasted the whole establishment of law and order! We were left with a garbled impression of a Dickensian prison cell with Jo's brother suffering a lingering death on a straw palliasse unattended and uncared for by doctor or warders. She had seen the solicitor and friends who had influence; there would be one hell of a showdown when the Press got to hear details of the neglect. And so it went on until even she began to wilt.

'You've had quite a day. Now it's bed for all of us.' Daphne's cool, level voice finally ended the tirade and I let down the bedflap and unrolled the bedrolls to hasten Jo's departure to the motor cabin. Sandra had left already.

'What do you think about the brother?' asked Daphne as we lay in bed.

I couldn't begin to surmise as we tried to conjecture what possible fragments of truth there could have been in the spate to which we had been subjected.

Suddenly there was a loud banging on the cabin side. 'Good *night.*' Jo's voice was harsh with suspicion and resentment. She had been listening to us through the partly opened slide over the hatch. Neither of us replied and from then on we avoided all mention of her when she was within any vicinity of the boats. I think we were both afraid of provoking an outburst from the emotional ferment which we sensed to smoulder always on the edges of her control.

6. The Lower Road

5 October. The narrow canal, now known as the Birmingham &
Fazeley, wound an oily route through the back end of the city
round to the Coventry coalfields. It was punctuated by a series of
single locks down to Tamworth, and it was a tedious business
taking a pair of empty boats through the stretch as we had to work
each boat separately through the locks.

Daphne explained that she and Jo would take the motor on
ahead and, as they left each lock, would close the bottom gate and
draw half a paddle so that the locks would fill by the time we
reached them with the butty. Sandra and I would take it in turns
to bowhaul, one to steer and one to pull.

It was raining. Those locks must have been – and probably still
are – some of the dirtiest on the Cut. The lock sides were greasy
with a thick, viscous, greenish-grey slime, and the towpath was
coated with coal-encrusted cinders. Inevitably the towing line
from the masthead became contaminated with the combination
of oil and cinders so that hands became chafed and roughened,
clothes were indescribably filthy and tempers fermented with
every delay or misjudgement. Sandra endured it all with stoic
endurance although the rough, jagged cinders must have been
crippling through the soles of her thin town shoes, and her feet
must have been cold and wet as she splashed along through the

murky pools which bogged the towpath at intervals. She said she hadn't seen any working boots without coupons in Birmingham and that she didn't have any coupons left. I began to admire her fortitude; my own was far more ephemeral! Why the hell shouldn't Jo be doing the bowhauling? Why us? Why me? I fumed and cursed the day I had ever thought of becoming a 'bargee'. I was nothing but a third-rate packhorse with the rope wound python-like over my shoulder and around my waist. I had relented towards Sandra when faced with her uncomplaining acceptance of the multitude discomforts and said that she should steer while I towed. My boots were reasonably proof against cinders and the wet, although my raincoat was ruined and becoming more porous by the minute.

'Daphne said they'd wait for us below the seven. Perhaps we'll change over then.' She was always so eager to placate all of us. Perhaps if I could have had a measure of her equanimity, I might have been spared the ensuing misfortune.

Few trainees escaped without accident. In Emma Smith's book *Maidens' Trip* (p. 199) the trainer's comments that one girl she was teaching broke her ankle and that another strained her heart were fairly typical examples of the casualty list among the women trainees. The collision of Charity's head with a passing bridge was ghoulishly retold and embellished by the crew of every pair of boats we met with on the locksides and in the pubs. The list of accidents and their severity increased as often as the tales were told!

It was inevitable that my turn would come! I was still too impetuous and anxious to prove my agility and competence, and the old training on the Return was still dominant. Hope's oft-repeated words, 'The boat first. We can't afford repairs,' were indelibly imprinted in my acquired precepts for boathandling and still dictated my reflexes during those early days on the canal boats. I was soon to learn the hard way that such a precept had no relevance on those seventy-footers and was soon to appreciate Miss Minn's disparaging comment at my interview that my experience on sailing boats would be of no use in my work on the canals.

Daphne and Jo had gone ahead with Capricorn and were soon out of sight. The rain continued in a steady, blanketing drizzle as I plodded along the length to the top of the next flight of downhill locks. Sandra stood at the tiller like Patience on her monument. The bowhauling wasn't hard work with the empty boat; once it was moving, the boat was carried by its own momentum and all I had to do was to maintain a walking pace with a steady pull on the rope. The top lock was in sight. I dropped the line and ran ahead to get the gate open for the on-coming butty. The lock was full but the gate wouldn't budge. I snatched the windlass from my belt and whipped up the nearest paddle to its fullest extent. The butty continued its passage down the channel in the middle of the Cut, and still the gate resisted my frantic efforts to get it open. There were only seconds before the boat would crash the gate.

'Get in to the side,' I yelled at Sandra, whose anxious face looked helplessly over the cabin top. 'Get over . . . over,' I yelled again but the crash was inevitable.

Then I did the most stupid thing it was possible to imagine. The old reflex took over, and it was the gate for which I was concerned. I had soon learned that to crash a gate on the Cut was the most heinous offence. I clambered onto the narrow ledge of the gate at the water level with some idiotic notion of being able to mitigate the impending impact. Luckily for me I slipped sideways as the bows charged the gate and, with the lock full of water, the gate merely shuddered. I had an arm looped around the iron guard at the top of the gate which saved me from a cold, oily immersion, and the boat missed me by inches. My left leg, however, had slipped into the water and was caught and twisted by the bows. Had it been the stem of the boat, the leg must have been broken. As it was, a doctor later diagnosed sprained collateral ligaments and I was immobilized for the rest of the trip.

Luckily, Daphne returned up at the side of the locks to see how we were doing and she helped me back onto the towpath. I couldn't stand and was in some pain, unable to get aboard the butty which Daphne had pulled into the side. Then Jo arrived. 'Thought something had gone wrong,' she said. Daphne explained that I couldn't get back on board.

Jo just picked me up – all ten stone of me – and lifted me into the well-deck of the butty. Later that evening we were to comment on the strength she had shown. I was forced to lie up in the cabin while the three of them took the boats round to Tamworth, where they were loaded with coal for Croxley papermills.

The journey back to Hawkesbury seemed endless. It was there that Daphne sent for a doctor as I was in considerable pain. He said I'd need an X-ray and proper treatment. I said that, if Daphne would agree, I'd wait until we reached London, where I lived. He wasn't interested and obviously thought us a feckless lot!

A passenger on training boats was a luxury we could ill afford and I tried to make amends by doing all the cooking with my leg stretched out along the side-bed. Many of the Diamond ranges, those most commonly fitted in the cabins, had a guardrail around the top to prevent kettles and pans sliding off, but for some reason the one on the range in Cleopatra was missing and I was constantly mopping up and grabbing at the red-hot handles to stave off disaster.

'Why do you bother?' asked Daphne after one of my moans. 'We can't eat it all anyway.'

As my concoctions were largely based on vegetables 'acquired' *en route* and tins of bully beef, she was right to refuse my generous helpings; eaten after a hard day's work, the results were noisy rather than nourishing!

Sandra withdrew more often to the motor cabin while Jo continued to spend her evenings in the butty.

'If only I could have hurt an arm instead of a leg,' I wrote, 'then I could have escaped from the endless noise of Jo's voice.'

At Braunston we tied up just beyond the entrance to Nurser's yard, where Daphne hoped to collect a painted water jug she had ordered a few weeks previously. We had finished supper and Daphne had sent Jo off, saying that we were going to bed. The boats were singled out and, reluctantly, Jo had gone striding off down the towpath. No sooner had she gone than there was a soft rap on the cabin side.

'You there, Daphne?' called a well-spoken voice.

Two blonde and beautiful sisters, looking as if they had come straight from the pages of *Vogue*, stepped down into the cabin. They had trained with Daphne and, after weeks, were still on their first working trip. They had broken down and no fitter had arrived to sort out the trouble.

'Could be the shafting,' said one of them. 'We caught the motor on the cill.'

I was fascinated by these two elegant young women who seemed so out of place on the canal boats. We nicknamed them 'the Dresden china girls', and in my diary they are referred to as 'the DCs'. It was a pleasant change to meet up with some of the other trainees for a good laugh and chat about people and events on the Cut. We had seen others but only in passing, and these were the first with whom there was time enough for a gossip. They had heard about my accident; news on the Cut travels fast.

'What happened about that person who swore all the time?' one asked, and 'Who else is with you? Any good?'

We chatted on easily and pleasantly, forgetful of Jo and Sandra. The scene was shattered rudely by the return of Jo, who had heard voices and come aboard.

12 October
. . . she came in to find them here. Very objectionable. Reviled D in the most disgusting manner, then flew out in a rage. D went out to look for her. The DCs horrified – returned to their boats. D & Jo returned – more cocoa to calm us all. The DCs returned to say that milk and margarine had been taken from their cabin. They accused Jo. Dreadful scene followed – vile abuse from Jo and threats to leave – which I hope will materialize. D has given milk and marg from our store to help pacify the girls. . . .
13 October
Complete change of mood. Jo obviously very sorry for all that happened. Swears it was a black-out and that she remembers nothing. Was Daphne mad at her? Was I mad at her? She expects me to sympathize – am terrified not to in case I provoke another flare-up of rage. Very exhausting. Poor Sandra. . . .

Jo had been with us for over three weeks and we were feeling the strain of her wild changes of mood and her demands on our time and emotions; the scenes with the DCs hadn't helped. I wondered at Daphne's tolerance and at Sandra's passivity. I withdrew, as far as possible, from all three during the following days. We would soon be back at the depot, where I would leave the boats for a spell of treatment to my leg, and Jo would have gone as crew to other boats by the time I returned. I have since wondered about the unfortunate Sandra, who left the boats as unobtrusively as she joined them. Sharing a cabin with Jo, even for the few hours of sleep, and being a quiescent spectator of all

Jo's tantrums and dominance as well as conforming to the demanding experience of living and working on the boats, must have been an unnerving period of endurance in her seemingly lack-lustre existence. She left the boats back at the depot, and neither Daphne nor I heard of her again.

Meanwhile we reached Croxley without further incident. Jo went off on some business of her own, saying that she'd hitch a lift to Watford and would be back that evening. Daphne and Sandra caught a bus to go shopping as we were not to be offloaded until the following morning.

I settled down to write letters and to enjoy the privacy of the cabin to myself. I was able to write up my diary and noted that I was glad to be sharing the cabin with Daphne if only it wasn't in constant use as a common-room by Jo and Sandra and 'others' we met with on the way! My knee was still painful and I was worried that some permanent damage might have been done which could prevent my continuing on the boats. Despite everything, I was more content and at ease than I had been for ages.

'Hallo there. Thought I'd come back to keep you company.' It was Jo, of course, and my heart sank. Her face peered through the open hatch and I knew there was no escape.

'I'm busy writing letters,' but my voice carried no conviction; even if it had, Jo would not have noticed. She was so completely immersed in her own needs and her own delusions that others existed only as receptors for her intensified emotions. 'Paranoia' and 'schizophrenia' were words unknown to either Daphne or myself at the time and, even had we guessed at her derangement as a recognizable form of illness, there would have been little we could have done to find a source of advice and treatment for her. Most of the time she seemed so rational and, above all, she was an excellent boatwoman. She was like quicksilver, seemingly solid but elusive with every point of contact.

'Never get to see you on your own,' she said closing the cabin doors behind her.

I panicked as she joined me on the side-bed and embraced me fiercely, trying to kiss me. She told me that, in fact, she was a man and that she loved me – had loved me since she had lifted me up on the lockside on the Lower Road. I was horrified and not a little frightened. My arms were pinioned and my leg hurt. I told her to get off my leg and then managed to dislodge myself from her embrace. Daphne and Sandra wouldn't be back for another hour at least. I had to keep her talking.

I got her to make tea as she told me something of her physical changes.

I write about Jo with some reluctance and trepidation but she made such an impact on those of us who knew her that she cannot be omitted from this account of our working lives on the Cut. In those days, when the residue of Victorian prudery enveloped most of us, such revelations seemed incredible and my efforts to talk with Jo about her dilemma would now seem very inhibited and pretentious.

Did Daphne know? I thought of all the hours Daphne had stood on the gunwale of the motor while Jo steered, and of her enigmatic comment that Jo 'had problems'.

'Asked Daphne to marry me,' said Jo. I swallowed hard at the thought. 'She refused me,' said Jo cheerfully, 'said I had to grow up first.'

She then proceeded to tell me again that I was the one she really loved. Remembering her outbursts of rage and jealousy, I was still fearful of offending her. Keep her talking . . . keep her talking . . . I asked her how she had passed the medical to come on the boats . . . what she had been doing before she had joined the boats . . . how had she got on with Sandra . . .what were the physical problems of such a change . . .

'Make some tea,' I said hastily as she stripped off her pullover to show me that her breasts were disappearing, 'Put on your pullover – it's cold.'

She busied herself and seemed easier now that she had told me. To my relief her amorous inclinations had subsided and she perched on the step while we drank our tea. She told me again of her achievements as an author and of her brother, who was feminine in his feelings and behaviour. I followed her leads into wild, disconnected accounts of her activities until, thankfully, I heard Daphne's voice from along the towpath.

We never knew quite what to believe in the strange, jumbled outpourings we endured for the rest of the trip.

20 October
Her mind is in the most awful state of chaos. . . . Flights of wild fantasy alternate with sanely bitter reflections on life and her own

misfortunes. Wild passions, fierce hates and a terrible suspicion of all our motives make her impossible to live with. Yet mixed up with these suspicions and passions is a good sense of humour, a great fund of kindness, protectiveness and generosity; and a great desire to give and accept affection – all of which make her very lovable at times. She is like an adolescent with every mood exaggerated. She is almost a man yet not enough developed either physically or emotionally to feel certain of himself in any way. . . . We feel terribly sorry for her but sometimes she really is too much for any normal person to deal with. We both feel rather at a loss.

In retrospect this reads like a gross under-statement!

Daphne was in a great dilemma as we discussed the problems late into the night, fearful always of being overheard by Jo. Whom would she work with and who would put up with her tantrums?

'She could be all right with someone who will stand no nonsense and let her have the motor cabin to herself.'

The answer came to us both simultaneously as we returned to the depot.

Margery was tough, super-efficient and silent; no one would take liberties with Margery, not even Jo. Also she preferred to live in the butty cabin which at present she was sharing with Kay, an equable and capable boatwoman not easily ruffled or alarmed. There was no reason to enlighten either Margery or Kay about Jo's 'condition'; rightly or wrongly we felt that it was Jo's affair. As long as she had the motor cabin to herself, no one need be embarrassed by Jo's difficulties.

Back at the depot Daphne talked over the proposition with Jo, and Jo agreed. I think she had been scared she would have to leave the boats. Daphne knew that Margery and Kay were working two-handed and guessed that Kay would welcome a third crew member. So it was arranged in the office that Jo would complete another trip on the training boats and then would join Margery and Kay. Margery had been contacted by phone and had agreed.

A solution had been found for Jo's problems – or so we hoped! – and I made a slow and laborious journey back to the sanctuary of my room in Chelsea. I could barely hobble even with the aid of a stout stick Jo had cut from a hedge and the pain did nothing to lighten my despondency at leaving the boats.

25 October
Still in London waiting through the days until I can go back to the boats. . . . I've been having massage, exercises and radiant heat treatment. Another week or so and I should be able to return to the boats.

Further entries indicate a busy round of visits despite the difficulties of walking:

Dinner with Frances, Kay and three Norwegians. Talked about education, underground movements – everything under the sun.
  Went to school – took a whole crowd of my ex-pupils for the last period – told them about the boats.
  Went to a lecture on Keats by Stephen Spender. I admired his high and noble brow!
  Anthony Hopkins played a sonata of his own – a game of speeds – fascinating.
  Scott Goddard gave a talk on Vaughan Williams. I might have appreciated it had it not been for S.G.'s mannerisms!
  Edmund Blunden was at Morley College and I heard him talk on Hardy. Very different from S.G. E.B. is small, clerk-ish, middle-aged, with nothing to distinguish him but his nervous, restless eyes. He has a dry, rather biting wit – often not understood by his audience!
  Went down to the boats with Kay. Wonderful to be back. Had supper with Daphne – then drinks in the pub. I join the boats next trip.

I read through even more entries of visits to friends and theatres and wonder what I did for money! Where could one go in London without a substantial bank balance, even in those days of austerity? (No DHSS hand-outs!) A brief entry indicates a temporary source of income: 'Have been to see John Vickers – photographic artist. I have promised to pose for him – £1 an hour – riches!' He paid me well and I was able to eat. I went to one of his parties but it wasn't my scene, and after I returned to the boats I forgot about him and his work.

7. Trainer's Mate

I rejoined Capricorn and Cleopatra at Southall early in November. My leg was now healed, although I still had to remember not to twist it in any way. No doubt the odd quirk reminding me of those weeks of near-immobility was to add the necessary degree of prudence and foresight to my expertise as a boatwoman.

Virginia was the only other trainee aboard and she was to start on her second training trip. There had been another recruit on her first trip who had decided to leave the boats for the Land Army. There was no one else on the waiting list, so there would just be the three of us. Daphne had heard nothing about Jo.

It was so good to be back again on the boats, away from the dirt and rubble of the bombed streets, away from the nightly yelping of the guns in Battersea Park, away from the talking – intellectual and trivial – with which I always seemed to be surrounded; and away from the complications of two uncertain and unsatisfactory relationships with which I was trying to patch up the emptiness left by J's death. Life on the boats opened a door of escape in the cage I had inadvertently created for myself. Daphne's smile of welcome was more heart-warming than Moshé's torrid embraces or Christopher's poetic declarations. I was so glad to be back.

It was a delightful trip and I savoured the pleasure that working with a regular and compatible crew could be. Virginia was easy-going and adaptable as well as being a very efficient boat-woman. She had been at Reading University but had left without finishing the course and had responded to the advertisement asking for women to work on the boats. She brought Candy with her, a silky white and golden spaniel bitch, to which she was devoted. Candy's beautiful coat and 'feathers' were more often a dirty grey than their original sleek elegance but she adapted speedily, if somewhat reluctantly, to the hazards of this strange existence.

We worked so well together that it was on this trip that the idea of having our own pair of working boats germinated. We would still need more experience and we'd also have to look out for a possible third trainee to crew. Then, as we came back down to Southall, Daphne asked me if I'd stay on as Trainer's Mate. She was getting rather tired of the continual change-over of new recruits, many of whom were totally unsuitable from the start. For some reason I did not mention that V and I were planning to have our own boats; probably, at the time, it would have seemed presumptuous. So I accepted Daphne's offer with alacrity. If I had to share a cabin, it would be far preferable to share with Daphne than with a total stranger.

Margery's boats were at the depot on our return, and there was Jo, ebullient as ever. She and Margery had worked two-handed as Kay had gone sick. Jo and Margery seemed to have survived well enough together. The work would have kept them fully occupied for at least twelve to fourteen hours of the day and, as each had a cabin, there was little need – or time – for any but the briefest of exchanges. The only controversy between the two had been over the steering. Margery regarded the motor steering as her prerogative and her responsibility, and Jo had been relegated to the butty, which I knew she disliked.

That evening the cabin was once again filled with the stridencies of Jo's voice and I was thankful that they would be off in the morning as Margery had orders to load at Brentford. Jo was introduced to Virginia and Candy, and then Margery joined us. She was a very aloof and self-contained person and there was no knowing whether or not she was aware of Jo's 'condition'. Probably not, we thought afterwards. Over the endless mugs of tea it was decided that Virginia would join them as their third crew member. She would share the butty cabin with Margery, and Jo would continue to have the motor cabin to herself. Virginia transferred herself and her few belongings and Candy to Margery's boats, and in the morning they had left before we were awake. It was always such a luxury to lie in while waiting for orders that we seldom surfaced before mid-morning.

Later that day we were joined by Helen, slightly built and elegant in her reefer jacket and yachting hat and good, tough shoes. The right gear at least, I thought, but, as we talked, I wondered how she would adapt to the muck and oil of the coalfields. She was a strange contrast to Jo and Peggy, and I found it hard to imagine her cleaning out the mudbox and the oil-filter, winding some of the very stiff paddle gear and using a bucket as the only form of lavatory. Later she told me how horrified she had been at the conditions in which we lived and worked but had decided that, if we could do it, so could she! Luckily for her there was no other trainee on her first trip so that she had the motor cabin to herself. Her husband was a Commander in the Royal Navy and, having no family, she had decided to try the boats in order to relieve the boredom during the long spells when he was away at sea. She was very 'county' and lent an air of respectability to the boats even on the worst days.

Helen compromised. She insisted on wearing gloves at all times to protect her hands, despite the fact that we were often furious with her when she missed or bungled a rope due partly to the gloves. She explained to Daphne that she would take leave from the boats whenever her husband was on leave, and this she did frequently (often when her husband was *not* on leave we guessed!), finding trains to Salisbury from isolated locations along the route and returning the same way. Daphne accepted Helen on her own terms as she had accepted all of us, each with her own quirks of personality and with peculiarities of needs and demands.

The two trips with Helen aboard went smoothly and without undue delays. I was becoming more proficient and confident with the work on the motor as well as on the butty so that Daphne was able to take the occasional 'restful' spell on the butty.

We came to Hatton on 17 November during that trip. Helen said she'd like to take the motor. How I envied and admired her confidence! But she was always more efficient with the powered boat than with the rope-handling and agility required for working the butty through the locks. It was obvious that Daphne would need to stay with the boats even though they were breasted up. My own confidence was still too irresolute and unreliable to compensate for Helen's lack of experience, so I offered to lock-wheel as the locks were all against us. I set off through the mud, the heavy mist and the gloom of a mid-November day. My old mac seemed more porous than ever, and the scarf around my head soon became a rain-sodden turban so that I stuffed it into a rain-sodden pocket. My hair needed a wash anyway! I worked up through the twenty-one, my mind blank and empty with the dull and heavy routine of winding paddles and opening gates. Finally I reached the top and looked back along the line of white-painted batons of the winding gear; the boats were still hidden in the thick mist of a darkening day. I should not have gone so far ahead! I slumped, exhausted, on the weather-grooved balance beam, impervious to the damp which penetrated every layer of my 'warm' clothing acquired in Limehouse and uncaring about what was happening to the boats below. I remembered Peggy and her outrage at such maltreatment of her muscles and stamina. Bloody gates, bloody paddles, I murmured in sympathy as I slid off the beam to lie exhausted and wretched on the wet grass. What a birthday!

The sound of a motor thumped my dulled senses back into action and I saw a pair coming through the bridge from the other direction. Why the hell couldn't they have come an hour earlier to have saved me the task of working at least half the flight? There was no one on the towpath, and it looked as if the boats were drawing in to the side; probably they were stopping for the night, hoping for a pair to come up in the morning so that there would be no need to lockwheel. It was the Smiths; they had wire round the blades at Catty Barnes, the steerer said, or they'd have been along an hour since! As the locks were ready, the man said they would go on down the locks – it would only take them an hour!

'Pair at the top,' I told Daphne as I went to help with the gates on the last-but-one lock. Helen was on the towpath and gasped, 'Lord, what a marathon. I could die.' I knew what she meant. Bloody gates . . . bloody paddles . . .

Daphne said we would tie up for the night as we reached the top; no one was in any state to go further. She and the Smiths exchanged news and pleasantries as Lil emerged reluctantly from the cabin, tying a mud-coloured scarf under her chin. George, her brother, helped us tie and then they were off.

I crossed over the rain-slippery gates with one hand firmly clasped to the rail. I didn't want another accident, and the ache in my knee emphasized the need for caution at all times. Helen had disappeared into the seclusion of the motor cabin. I lowered my weary wet length into the butty cabin, where Daphne was sitting on the side-bed wiping off her steamed-up specs. 'D'you think you could get some more coal?' she asked.

Ungraciously I took the bucket to fill it from the bunker, an awkward job to grovel under the protecting planks for the diminishing pile at the bottom of the boat and, as I leaned over, the boat gave a lurch which jerked my knee so that I shouted in rage and pain, 'Why me? Why do *I* have to fill the blasted bucket? I'm nothing but a serf . . .'

What a birthday! A great sense of injustice and self-pity flooded through me as I lowered myself into the bunker and filled up the bucket easily.

'You all right?' called Daphne from across the cabin top. I didn't answer. 'Let me take the bucket,' she said, coming round to the side of the boat. 'I've made the tea.'

I handed up the bucket, heaved myself up from the bunker and limped my way behind her to the cabin. After all, she didn't know it was my birthday!

'How's the leg?' she asked. I thought she had forgotten.

I wrote up my diary while Daphne washed up and then crossed over to see if Helen was all right. When she returned, I was dozing in the comfort of my sleeping-bag and pretended to be asleep.

On our way to Knowle the next morning we met the Beresford 'boys' – two brothers who, probably, were too young to be in the forces and who worked the boats with their father.

'Knowle's ready for you,' called out the one on the motor. 'Any coming behind you?'

It was a rhetorical question, as they always knew the movements of most of the boats. I saw Daphne shake her head and call out that the Smiths had gone down Hatton the previous evening. Helen and I were on the butty and we just smiled and waved as the boats passed each other. Helen asked me if we saw much of the other women who were on the boats. I told her there were only about six pairs crewed by women as most left after a year or two at the most and that I had only met up with Margery and Kay, with Emma and her crew and with Audrey, Evelyn and Anne, who were tied up in an arm just below Cowley where they were supposed to be making a film of the working boats (*see* Pl. 4). I knew they were fed up with the days and weeks of inactivity and would have preferred to be back working. Helen wondered which boats she would join after her two training trips.

'D'you think you'll stay?' I asked sceptically.

'Will you stay?' she replied with some asperity.

'Yes,' I replied briefly and knew that I would.

She was steering the butty under my instruction and surprised me by the strength she displayed in rowing round some of the bends. She knew that I was deceived by her appearance and enjoyed pre-empting my advice. I retreated to the cabin to make mugs of cocoa before we should reach the locks.

And at Knowle there was Harold – Harold Stocker.

18 November

A boy of nine or ten was waiting by the bottom lock. Filthy face and hands. He came up the locks with us, closing and opening the gates. He told us that he lived nearby and asked if he could come with us to Birmingham to visit his grandmother. He said he would ride his father's bike back the next day. So we took him and put him off on the towpath when we reached Tyseley. Later we went to the cinema and returned very late to find Harold waiting for us with a bunch of chrysanthemums. He said that they were from his granny and that it was too dark to find his way back to her house. We were in a fix. What could we do with him? We took him over to the nightwatchman, a great lazy hulk who was no help at all.

We decided to take him to find his grandmother, although we began to doubt her existence. In the darkness on the slippery towpath Harold disappeared. We were both so dead tired that we then decided to phone the police and return to the boats. The public phone was out of order, so we knocked up a shopkeeper, who insisted that it cost 2d every time we dialled the operator! He had on only one shoe, and dirty toes protruded from an old sock on the other! We were glad to get away although we hadn't managed to contact the police. Later, when we had flopped into bed, I thought I heard footsteps on the cabin roof. I called out but there was no answer; Daphne was asleep and I was too tired to investigate.

The next morning Helen found Harold asleep on the coal in the bunker. He was dirty, cold and hungry. Helen and I gave him breakfast while Daphne went to contact the police. It was obvious that there was no grandmother, no goats, no home. He cried when the police came for him; they thought he must have run away from 'school'. I must ring up the police when we get to Coventry to find out what has happened to him.

Whether or not I did ring the police I have no recollection and, sadly, I have no idea what happened to Harold, yet another refugee from the harshness of life who thought that the boats would provide sanctuary and a solution to his problems. There had been Mary, Jo and Harold in the space of just a few weeks.

We offloaded our cargo of coal at the Nestlé factory below Cowley and then had orders to return with empty boats to the coalfields. Only one incident is recorded for that return trip, otherwise all must have gone smoothly.

1 December
It has been cold but sunny, a winter's day at its best, and I enjoyed the run from Stoke to Buckby where we are now tied. The only mishap occurred in Blisworth tunnel. I was on the motor, Helen down in her cabin and Daphne was on the butty. We were well into the darkness when the headlight went out. The light from the butty wasn't too good either as the battery was on its second day; we had forgotten to change it over for charging. Daphne shouted from the butty but there was little she could do. Helen came up with a small torch and held it over the side from the empty hold. To make matters worse, the light suddenly went on at intervals for just long enough to dazzle me before it went off again. We managed quite well and without even a bump! Must look for that loose connection.

I really came to enjoy travelling through the tunnels. They were warm and dry (more or less!) in winter and pleasantly cool in the heat of summer. Blisworth and Braunston, although almost two miles in length, were high and wide and well maintained.

Many years later, when on holiday in our 'noddy' boat, we traversed the Harecastle tunnel and I found the journey far more intimidating. The roof came down low over the cabin roof so that I had to crouch while my son Giles splashed along the sunken and broken towpath to try to keep the boat from becoming wedged in the narrow channel. Then, as others who have travelled the Harecastle will remember, the sides of the tunnel suddenly disappeared into black, empty spaces where pockets of old mining activities made us realize that this tunnel must once have been a busy highway. It took us almost two hours before we again emerged into the daylight, black with muck from the oily water and the dirty sides of the tunnel. We crawled into the shelter of the Macclesfield arm to repair the paintwork and the damage to our nerves!

There were always stories about the tunnels: a cow fell into the Cut at one end of the Preston Brook tunnel on the Bridgewater canal and swam three-quarters of a mile to emerge at the further end none the worse for its immersion. We only *heard* of the episode, as our boats never worked the extensive network north of Brummagem and Coventry. We often wished to go exploring but that pleasure was delayed for me for almost another twenty years.

In our own time there was the story of the trainee who lost the butty in Braunston tunnel. The light on the butty had failed – another loose connection? – and the steerer on the motor failed to realize that the butty was no longer in attendance until she emerged from the tunnel. We secretly thought that the steerer must have been somewhat unobservant not to have missed the pull of the butty! Three years later, at the reunion dinner for 'bargees' in Bad Salzuflen, Stella from Hyperion and Capella told the story with great zest and many embellishments!

'Olga was on the butty,' she told me amid the applause, 'and I had it direct from her. They were terrified,' she added. So it was true after all; until then I think I hardly believed it. My own mishap in Blisworth seemed very tame by comparison!

Gradually my 'step sideways' took more purposeful strides into the learning and lore of our nomadic existence. We came to know every bridge'ole where the lockwheeler would step off from the narrow gunwale, bicycle in hand, to go shopping in a nearby village store; the water depths at every tie-up where we could moor the boats either breasted up or singled out, loaded or empty, we were soon able to gauge to a nicety. We used the recognized stopovers where there were rings or stakes set into

1. Women man the boats at the wharf just past the depot at Bull's Bridge. Cetus was butty to Hercules and Hyperion. The boat in the foreground is loaded with aluminium bars

2. 27 years old and new to the boats

3. Some of the women trainees. Emma Smith, author of *Maidens' Trip* is second from the right and Stella is on her right. Olga is on the far left and Daphne French is just behind

4. Audrey, Evelyn and Anne on the boats Sun and Dipper. Trainer Kit in her distinctive cap is leaning on the butty tiller

5. Helen concentrating hard as she takes the motor out of a downhill lock

6. Freddie Einengler, a professional photographer, took this photo of me, Helen (posing with the shaft), Virginia (on the right) and her spaniel Candy as we were tying up Hercules and Cetus at Leighton Buzzard. He came on board for a 'holiday' and we put him to sleep on the coal under the for'ard cratch!

7. Young Rosie Skinner on Jo Skinner's boat the Friendship. Note the rose-and-castle decoration and the decorated water can

8. A pair loaded with coal on the Bridge-water canal – the butty is towed on a seventy-foot length of snubber

9. Trainer Daphne on the Cleopatra

10. Audrey with a long shaft on the Dipper

11. A procession of loaded boats waiting to lock through during the ice-up

12. Helen and I (at the tiller) at Hawkesbury Stop

13. (*above*): Evelyn and Anne of the Sun and Dipper

14. (*left*): New Zealander Cicely and Kay

15. (*below*): Virginia (*top*), Candy and I take leave from the boats – and go punting!

My own boat. 16. (*above*): The Alphons as a working butty in Cassiobury Park. 17. (*below*): M. Ridout & Co. (my married name) moored at Stowe Hill wharf where much of this book was written

concrete. We didn't carry mooring stakes, as the use of them was considered detrimental to the banks. Every twist and turn of the channel, kept open by the constant passage of the boats, was recognized; to deviate from the channel was to get embedded in the pile-up of mud at the sides of the canal or on the inside of a bend.

On the return trip with Daphne and Helen, we tied at the top of Knowle, probably to enquire about young Harold.

7 December
Yesterday we went down to Knowle, a charming village with streets of old houses. We had tea in the Creswolde Arms; the comfort and rest were a welcome respite. Then we visited an old antique shop kept by the Pickerings, a delightful, elderly couple. We looked at their lovely possessions and then sat by their fire munching home-made cakes and talking of problem children. We told them about Harold.

Evidently there was no news of the boy and we could only guess at his uncertain future.

At Croxley, where we were offloaded, we were held up for a day as one of the heavy gates was jammed and we had to wait for help as all our prodding with the long shaft and letting down rushes of water were of no avail. One of the few BWB men still available came with his long, pronged shaft and removed a large brick which had been dislodged from the side of the lock and had become jammed against the cill at the bottom opening of the chamber.

The depot was deserted. We heard that Margery's boats were tied at Brentford and that they had gone on leave. We were also due for leave. Helen had completed her two training trips and decided that she would take an extended leave to spend Christmas at her home near Salisbury. Before she left, I asked her if she would care to join Virginia and myself on our own pair of boats. She said she wasn't too anxious to go as crew with strangers as the work was too exacting and the living too confined! Meanwhile she'd enjoy the luxuries of a more civilized way of life until I contacted her.

Daphne had relatives in London, and I looked forward to baths, a comfortable bed and meetings with old friends.

A few days of such 'civilized' living were enough for me and I was beginning to feel restless and to wonder where I would spend Christmas when Daphne phoned.

'How do you feel about returning to the boats?' she asked. I was more than delighted. Miss Minn had phoned her to say that a new recruit was anxious to join the boats as soon as possible. Her home had been demolished by a direct hit, and her parents had been killed.

'Her name is Elsie; that's all I know,' said Daphne. 'Meet you at the boats day after tomorrow.'

I was sceptical about Elsie's credentials for joining the boats. More problems? However, I now felt proficient enough to work two-handed with Daphne if necessary and we could easily accommodate a beginner, however helpless. But Elsie was far from helpless. She was short and sturdy with burn marks on her face, and she wore specs. She was tough and enduring and if she grieved for the loss of her parents it was only in the privacy of her cabin. Her 'uniform' was a pair of wellington boots and an old tweed coat, and I can still see her at the butty tiller enjoying the thrill of being a traveller despite the cold and the hunger pangs from which we all suffered. She was an excellent boatwoman, although, like Eileen, she was reluctant to take the motor and preferred either to lockwheel or to steer the butty. I lost touch with her after she left the boats but I feel certain she never regretted her experience of exchanging her life as a dressmaker for that of a canal boatwoman.

By 24 December we were tied up at Griff Colliery near Nuneaton and I had time to write up my battered-looking diary.

24 December
Christmas Eve and we're sitting peacefully in the cabin. Have been busy decorating the boats with evergreens and berries – some painted! – We are tied up by a deserted colliery on a small arm off the canal. There is another pair tied below us but no sign of life. The land is flat and dreary – a muddy lane leads to a distant road. A low, clammy mist covers everything and penetrated only by a strong smell of goats which are tethered on the nearby mounds.

We had previously walked into Nuneaton and ordered ourselves a Christmas dinner at the Newdigate Arms. On Christmas Morning we made great efforts to conform to the remembered norms of respectability. We filled the cans with water, stoked up the fires and washed hair and bodies in turn. Daphne found an old flat-iron and we pressed our more respectable pairs of trousers. Pullovers and blouses were dragged from the drawers and inspected for holes and smells. None of us had the luxury of a dress.

Very clean and hopeful, we walked through the deserted streets to the large, Victorian hotel. Immediately we knew we had made a mistake. We were 'bargees' and, even though there was a war on, trousers and pullovers were not the regulation dress for Christmas dinner in an hotel! We were put in the gloomiest corner of a great gloomy room with the tables so far apart that we were surrounded by our own isolation. We talked in hushed whispers, conscious that every word was amplified in that respectable gloom. We didn't even order drinks; as I tended to get rather verbose after a couple of sherries, Daphne said we had better wait until later!

We had a bottle of rum and another of brandy back on the boats. The hilarity of the rest of that Christmas Day more than compensated for the tedium of sitting through that hotel dinner. We sang every carol we could think of – the same verses over and over to make up for words we had forgotten. With the range fire roaring and the cabin doors open to the starry night sky, we were oblivious to the standards of decorum and respectability of the world 'out there'.

We enjoyed a couple of days' rest and then were loaded with coal, wheeled up in barrows along planks stretched from the bank up into the hold. It was a tedious and protracted method of loading and we were kept busy most of the time with our shovels to level the coal as the men tipped it in from their barrows. On the way south again to Langley Mills we had a breakdown at the top of Itchington which delayed us for two days and then the butty 'ellum came off in one of the locks so that *we crawled into a Barlow depot to be repaired as the retaining pin was badly bent.*

Back at Bull's Bridge there was an unexpected change of plans. There were two new recruits, friends, who were waiting to join the boats. Kit, the other trainer, already had three and we had met them on their way up to Tyseley. As it happened, Susan and Cicely, who had been working two-handed, were also overnighting at the depot and, over hurried discussions, it was agreed that

115

Elsie would join them so that we could take the two new ones. Elsie was somewhat apprehensive but Susan was a friendly soul who soon reassured her. Daphne promised her that she could return to the training boats if and when she felt the need. They were off immediately, northwards, and we had orders to pick up a load of fencing stakes from Brentford. They were all ready for loading so it would be a quick turn-around, and the two new girls would meet us at the depot the following day.

The weather had already turned very cold, and Daphne hung the hurricane lantern in the engine-room at night in case of frost. And frost and ice there was for the rest of January, through that memorable winter of 1945. Rosalie and Josephine (not another Jo!) joined us at the depot on our return. No one could have chosen a worse time to come aboard for their first trip on the canals and, no doubt, they remember it as one of the most traumatic experiences of their young lives.

On the third day out we knew from our steaming breath in the cabin, from the layer of frozen condensation on walls and roof and from the crawling cold of our feet at the ends of our sleeping-bags that the bright, glittering frost would sparkle back at us when Daphne pushed open the cabin door. 'Thick,' she said, hastily re-closing the door and poking hopefully at the fire. She pulled on a jersey over her pyjamas while her lower half remained encased in the comparative warmth of the blankets. I buried my nose again and drew up my knees. Not for long; I knew I would have to emerge sooner rather than later! We swallowed the scalding tea and Daphne said she would go over to the other cabin to see if the other two had kept the fire in.

She went out carefully and put a leg over the butty side to the motor counter.

'It's like glass,' she called out. A minute later she came back for sticks and coal. Our new recruits were an improvident pair. They remained cloistered in the cabin while Daphne and I prized open the hard, frozen ropes and threw them over the cabin top and the cratch in the hope that they would thaw out in the glimmer of sun. The small heat from the hurricane lantern made a surprising difference to the temperature in the engine-room, and Capricorn's engine coughed into life at our first attempt. I thought that the thump of the engine might have spurred the two girls into action but there was no response, so we set off, with Daphne on

116

the motor and me on the butty. Daphne had lit the fire in the motor cabin while the girls shivered over breakfast.

The boats moved slowly and creakingly through the thin ice until we reached the bottom of Hatton. The locks were against us, and that would mean at least three hours of solid work for everyone on the training boats. Rosalie had now emerged and I saw Daphne tuck a windlass into her belt and hand over the motor's tiller. 'Breast up in the lock,' she called back to me. The bows of the motor were in the mouth of the lock, and the butty, on half a length of snubber, was braked with its nose in the ice. Even the swirl of water for emptying the lock would do little to move the boats held in the channel by the thicker ice near the banks, and I dived down into the cabin for a couple of minutes' warmth and to make us some cocoa. A shout shot me straight back up the step to the deck, from where I saw Daphne floundering in the water. Thank God the engine was in neutral, I thought, as I hoisted myself onto the cabin roof. The butty's stern was well out from the bank and I would have to crawl along those slippery top planks. Rosalie's shouts continued to echo back from the blank wall of the closed lock gates as I climbed gingerly down onto the foredeck. Daphne was clutching at the stone coping and I saw with relief that she was still wearing her specs and had managed to throw her windlass onto the concrete. But I knew she hadn't a hope of getting out: the water was deep there in the mouth of the lock.

'Pull in the tow-rope,' I yelled to Rosalie. She heard me through her panic and pulled on the frozen, dripping rope; handling it must have been murder, and the ice, although not thick, added further resistance to her efforts. Josephine now appeared and lent her strength so that the bows of the butty nudged the fenders of the motor and I was able to clamber across.

'Coming,' I shouted to Daphne as I heaved myself onto the roof of the motor cabin. Capricorn had slewed away from the side so that the boats were near enough for me to get off. I straddled the top planks until I could lower myself and step onto the coping. Rosalie had resumed her shouting and was now reinforced by Josephine, who later said she'd never been so terrified in her life. I lay flat and grabbed at Daphne's wrists but it was no good. Her waterlogged coat and the depth of the water made it impossible to get her out. Worse, the motor was beginning to slew back again so that there was danger of its crushing her against the side.

'Get on the cabin top and push off with the shaft,' I yelled.

But their screams had been heard. A man appeared with a great pronged trident over his shoulder. 'Grab hold of that,' he shouted, pushing the handle at Daphne.

Between us we dragged the soggy bundle onto the bank. After a few gasps she managed to stand and said that the water hadn't really reached her skin as she had on too many clothes! Then she retreated to the warmth of the engine-room as the man pulled the boat alongside with his trident. Rosalie too was stirred to action by the rescue and offered to go below and brew up.

'Lucky your mates have some good lungs,' said our friend. He had been clearing the ice, had seen the boats coming and heard the shouts. 'Miss French, isn't it? Not often she goes in,' he said with respect in his voice.

He drew the butty up alongside the motor with his trident and I was able to hand Daphne some dry clothes and then to tie the boats at bows and sterns. The lock-keeper helped us up through the lock, and soon we were at the top, laughing and warming hands around the mugs of cocoa. I thought of my own immersion weeks earlier and was thankful it had not been in such icy and difficult conditions. Quits, I thought with a slightly malicious relish; Daphne had proved as vulnerable to accidents as myself!

She was none the worse for her near-disaster but the incident had scared the two girls badly. We struggled on to Tyseley where the stakes were offloaded and we restored our morale with baths, cinema and a café supper of sausages and chips. The meat content of the sausages was minimal but we didn't care; they looked like sausages and were off the ration, and we enjoyed eating them in the thick, smoky warmth of the dockside caff.

The ice and cold had not finished with us and, as we set out with empty boats for Braunston and the coalfields, the temperature fell perceptibly, not only in the weather but in the relationship between us and the new recruits. At Tyseley Daphne had asked them if they wanted to stay on and, to our surprise, they had said they did. However, after the first few hours from Tyseley it became evident that their decision to stay was for some obscure reason we could not understand. We struggled on during those final days before the ice-up almost two-handed.

8 January
Our difficulties have not been lightened by the two trainees. J, who at first seemed to be bright and enthusiastic, has turned out to be a ceaseless grumbler. She does nothing and stays in the cabin unless called out, then disappears again as soon as possible. She grumbles about the work, the food, the cold (not surprisingly!), her digestion, the cabin – everything. She infects R, who might have been good on her own . . .

All the way from Tyseley we struggled to keep going, using the motor as an ice-breaker. We unhitched the butty, took the motor ahead on full throttle for short bursts to break up the ice and, when a passage had been cleared, returned for the butty. It was a tedious procedure and, with empty boats high up out of the water, not very efficient. The locks at Warwick and Long Itchington were well encased by solid sheets of ice by the time we reached them. To clear the chambers of ice so that the gates could, with great effort, be opened on their frozen bearings, we had first to break up the ice and then to prod the hunks of it from behind the gates with the long shafts and, when the gates were opened, to shift as much of the ice as possible out into the channel. We called the shafts 'poles-in-aspic' as the Cut water froze into layers of ice which soon encased them from end to end. It was useless to wear gloves as they soon got soaked and froze to our hands. The danger of slipping made every move precarious, and hands stuck to the frozen guardrails on the lock gates.

Helen had chosen a good time for her extended Christmas leave!

We had seen no other boats; the Cut was deserted. Another day and we would have made it to Braunston! Finally we made it to the Blue Lias – lonely and desolate in those days – where at least we were within reach of a water supply. The ice gripped us at last and, with some relief, Daphne decided that we could go no further.

'There's a station half a mile down the road,' she said to Rosalie and Josephine as they shared the stew I had made. She hoped they would offer to go but they ate on in silence.

Very early the next day, however, while it was still dark, we heard movements.

'They're going,' I whispered. We listened in the darkness and felt sorry for them. The motor was tied on the outside and they would have to cross over the butty to get onto the bank. Had they been just slightly more communicative, we gladly would have helped them. As it was, they struggled with their bags while we listened to them leave. Later I was to write: *'We were neither surprised nor sorry. They left the motor cabin in the most filthy mess; the smell was horrible.'*

During the week long that we were tied up I had plenty of time to record my impressions of those wintry days.

The ice has kept us for a whole week tied near the Blue Lias, the only sign of habitation. For the first two days we were so exhausted that we just stayed in bed and slept. We had wonderful ideas about getting all the odd jobs done but it's surprising how few have been accomplished. Each morning the ice around the boats has to be broken to keep the boats afloat. The shafts are as cold as ever!

Over a very late breakfast after the flight of Rosalie and Josephine we tried to review the disasters of the trip and to decide what more we could have done to help the newcomers survive the ordeals which had defeated them. We were glumly despondent, from exhaustion and feelings of failure and also from the fact that our coal supply was almost at an end. The last scrapings from the bunker were producing more smoke than heat. On our previous trip south we had carried coal too fine for use on our ranges, and our reserves had dwindled slowly as we travelled northwards again to Tyseley and back towards Braunston. If only we could have reached Braunston, where we knew there would be other boats tied up against the ice!

'What about asking Amy at the pub?' I suggested.

We knew that Amy's supplies would be limited. The Blue Lias was very isolated and, with the state of the roads, delivery of fuel and supplies would have been uncertain. We decided to ask only if absolutely desperate.

'We'll take a look along the banks,' said Daphne.

It wasn't unusual to see a pile of coal left by passing boats to be collected by a previous arrangement with another pair, such as ourselves, who weren't carrying domestic coal. Normally no one except those for whom the coal was designated would dream of taking the reserved fuel, but these were not normal conditions and we were feeling desperate. Reluctantly we emerged into the crisp white snow, and the fine, cold air was infinitely preferable to the smoky chill of the cabin once we had made the effort. Neither of us felt very hopeful but it was better to be doing something than to be sitting around moaning at our predicament. We'd collect whatever sticks we could find and hope to dry them on the top of the range with the residue of heat from the wretched fire.

Then Daphne made a find. She discovered a large pile of coal below the next lock, well back from the bank and almost hidden by the scrubby bushes. It was too large a pile to have been left as a refill for coalboxes, although, no doubt, it had been 'delivered' by boat. There were many transactions on the Cut, and coal, good domestic coal, was a valuable commodity for barter.

We didn't stop to ask questions or to wonder who might claim it or even to doubt our own right to help ourselves. We collected buckets and filled them from that lovely store of frost-covered coal. We filled up the coalbox in the motor cabin and had almost filled the one in the butty when an irate lock-keeper appeared and accused us of stealing *his* coal.

Years later, when I was on a visit to Daphne in her home near Wicklow, we had a good chuckle as we remembered the incident.

'Caught red-handed, weren't we?' said Daphne. 'Remember how we pleaded, offered to pay?'

'You told him it was a question of survival.' The words had come dredging up from my submerged memories.

'So it was, so it was,' said Daphne fervently. 'But we had the last laugh after all. Remember?'

The lock-keeper had been obdurate: the coal would have to be returned. Ignominiously we carried the coal, bucket by bucket, back from the butty cabin to the precious heap while he stood and watched. He threatened us with 'proceedings' if we should attempt to touch his coal again – and he'd be down every day to keep an eye on us! Finally he went and we retreated back to the butty cabin suitably humiliated. Then we looked at each other and grinned – the coalbox in the motor cabin was still full of his precious coal, neither of us had made the slightest move to shift it back again to his pile! There was plenty to keep us warm for a few evenings at least.

'I also seem to remember taking a trip or two by moonlight,' I said.

Forty years later we were both laughing at the memory of two grown women, a bucket of coal in each hand, being accused and berated by a parsimonious lock-keeper.

'I only hope his need was as great as ours,' observed Daphne as we drank tea in the comfort of her sitting-room.

'By day we padlocked the cabins so that he would think we had left and walked into Leamington.'

'We could only light the fire after dark when we knew he'd be safe at home.'

I showed her the article I had written for *Waterways World* (February 1980) which recalled details of that memorable trip.

'Those two,' she said referring to Rosalie and Josephine, 'How on earth do you remember their names?'

I showed her the journal in which I had made my sporadic entries and read out a further excerpt written in those far-off days:

Each day we padlock the cabins and hitch or walk into Leamington where we enjoy the luxury of hot baths or go to the cinema where it is warm! We always have tea in the Pump Room where Van der Venn's trio play all our requests. We feel obliged to spend part of every evening in the Blue Lias where, in return for the use of their pump, we drink the very cold beer in their very draughty kitchen.

Eventually we were rescued by the ice-breaker which cleared a passage for us at the top of the locks; the kindly crew also helped us through. We followed them to Braunston and, as the channel was more or less clear of ice, we continued two-handed to Hawkesbury.

8. Two-Handed

There were no more new recruits waiting when Daphne phoned Miss Minn. Mr Vieter at the office said that we would load at Longford and that another cold snap was predicted.

It was still very cold but, although there was a thin coating of ice on the canal each morning, it was melted by a warm sun, and there was no wind. We thought we'd make it easily to Braunston and from there southwards we'd be in the main stream of the traffic.

'What about using the towing line?' I suggested. 'Easier for both of us.'

Daphne was hesitant, 'Can be dangerous . . . no more accidents.'

There were several advantages in the use of the towing line as an alternative to the direct stern-to-foredeck strap or snubber, and it was used by most of the boatpeople as a more efficient method of steering a loaded butty even through most of the locks. The pull was from the butty masthead (*see* Pl. 16) where the towing line was passed through a pulley to run the whole length of the hold through blocks firmly attached to the top planks. It was finally secured by the butty steerer with a figure-of-eight and a half-hitch to a stud on the cabin roof. This gave control of the towing line to the butty steerer, who could shorten or lengthen it as required. If the boats suddenly had to brake, the steerer could throw off the towing line from the motor and it would be pulled in by the butty steerer. So often, when the motor braked by going astern, the towing line would slacken and droop overboard and under the motor counter to get entangled in the turning blades. To keep control of the steering and the gearwheel in a tight situation often meant that the steerer forgot to pull in the lengthening slack of the towing line – especially on the training boats! It was also much easier to steer a loaded butty with the bows free from the direct pull of the strap or snubber. But there was a snag: with the towing line there was always the danger for the less dextrous of catching fingers, even hands, in the rope around the stud as it tightened. First-timers on the training boats had neither the necessary experience nor the expertise to use the towing line with either safety or expediency, and so I had never had the opportunity for using the more workman-like towing line.

'Just don't catch your hand in the line. Let it go rather,' said Daphne. 'It's the one danger you have to watch for as the line tightens.'

It was the most trouble-free trip I had so far experienced on the training boats, despite a further hold-up in a line of boats heading south from Braunston. The cold snap predicted by Mr Vieter returned as a final challenge to test the thin reserves of stamina and energy. The channel was kept open by the constant passage of the boats, but within the closed walls of the locks the ice once again solidified to make progress difficult. Happily for us, there were now plenty of men armed with their 'poles-in-aspic' on the locksides to prod at the chunks of ice and to free the ice-bound bearings on the gates so that, although we queued in a line of boats to go through each lock, we could wait our turn in the warmth of the cabin. Although we kept the fire in the motor cabin alight during the day for the comfort of the steerer, we let it out at night to conserve our fuel. We continued to share the butty cabin for the purpose of economy and because we couldn't be bothered to make any change in our established routine.

One incident is recorded in my diary which slightly moderated my pleasure in that return trip. It concerned one of the more intimate necessities of daily living. The bucket was our only form of lavatory and it was kept in the engine-room and used there; it was also used for baling the bilges, swabbing down and emptying the old oil after an oil change! I remember a good laugh on a later trip at the vision of an oily ring on Susan's bottom on one of our infrequent strip-down washes; upon inspection, mine too carried the mark! On the dark, cold evenings it was often too much of an effort to clamber round to the engine-room and we kept a spare bucket in the cabin to spare ourselves the effort. The two galvanized metal flanges into which the bucket handle was slotted were uncomfortable; and the menace of the great unprotected flywheel imposed both speed and care as we struggled with our layers of clothing through the winter months. The bucket-and-chuck-it method of disposal was used by all boaters and trainees although the over-the-side was so discreetly performed that only once was I caught in the act. This was on our present two-handed trip south when we were again delayed by ice through the locks below Berker. Today, of course, sanitary-disposal stations are provided throughout the canal network.

Our progress through the locks was slow but not too exacting with all the male muscles to shift the ice and move the gates. By the end of the second day the temperature began to improve, and on the morning after we had tied the boats by the Glaxo factory where we would be offloaded Daphne opened the cabin door and sniffed – 'No frost,' she said. Over a late breakfast we felt quite cheerful; our moods fluctuated with the weather! There was still plenty of ice sheeting the sides of the canal but the channel was free, and a hesitant sun gave our spirits a lift.

'We'll fill up the boxes and the bunker now that we have some decent coal,' said Daphne. 'Better get going before the men come to unload.'

We shovelled away at the life-saving fuel; without any feelings of guilt we made sure there would be sufficient for our needs throughout the next two trips. There would be no recurrence of our plight at the Blue Lias just two weeks previously.

Back at the depot there was a message that we should wait there for a couple of days until two more recruits came to join us. Daphne suggested I take some leave but I felt disinclined to pick up threads of relationships which were beginning to pall and which seemed so superficial viewed from a basic survival existence on the boats. I offered to stay and do some necessary repairs on the fenders. I enjoyed working with rope; I liked the smell and the feel of the cotton, the hemp and the sisal. There would be loose ends and pieces I could scrounge from the workshops. Daphne said she would have a go at the stern gland and clean up the engine. She knew that engine maintenance was one of my less favourite jobs.

Gradually I learned some of the more basic requirements of service to the National engine with which our boats were fitted. There were still plenty of old Bolinders around, easily recognizable by their steady thump, but on the trainees' boats water-cooled engines were fitted. Engine maintenance was an experience alien to most of us born in an age when cars and engines were still exciting innovations. To me, the most important component of that vast metal hunk were the two brass pumps which reminded me of the empty shell casings kept as souvenirs from the 1914–18 war. Upon their maintained action depended the level of the bilges; if the level rose for just a few inches, the menace of the turning flywheel would spray the greasy, oily fluid into every corner and over every surface in seconds. The smallest piece of grit or coal granule finding its way through the outer casing would be sufficient to impede their alternating rhythms. One experience of an oil-drenched engine-room was a sufficient deterrent to ensure that the function of the pumps became top priority on my list of essential duties to the chores of the engine-room. To clean out the pumps, the top half of the cylindrical tube was unscrewed and a length of rigid wire with a blob of grease on the end was inserted into the narrow aperture to which any foreign body would adhere and could then be withdrawn. It was often necessary to repeat this performance several times before the thin trickle of 'water' again flowed freely from the outlet in the hull.

The mudbox was another of the less attractive engine-room chores. This was the filter for the water-cooling intake from the Cut, and it was always full of grey, greasy slime which we emptied on the bank. Then the mudbox was thoroughly rinsed and cleaned for the following week.

'Come and help me lift the flooring,' called Daphne from the engine-room. Reluctantly I left my half-made fender in the warmth of the cabin.

Daphne was in stained and worn dungarees with her hair tied up in a scarf. There were smudges of oil on her face, and her hands were filthy. We were tied up near the tap on the bank and I

126

had filled the water jugs and had the kettle boiling on the range ready for when she would have finished. We lifted the heavy steel plates of the engine-room flooring between us and eased them out through to doors onto the bank; they would have to be scrubbed with Vim and wire wool. It was an exhausting 'rest' day! We compensated that evening with a supper of fish and chips and a visit to the cinema in Southhall – for us the ultimate in luxury!

There was yet another morning's work to be tackled but there was no sense of the urgency which usually accompanied such chores. The new trainees would not arrive until the next morning and, on one of those days which prelude a promise of spring after the bitter days of the winter, it was good to be working on the boats, good to get them into working trim ready for the next trip. I pulled out the Brasso and rags to polish portholes, chimney chains and all the brass appurtenances of the engine, so that I left the engine-room doors open for any passing boatman to see the sun glint on my efforts. I finished the tipcat to replace the old drooping and shredded apology on the stern of the motor, then patched up the front fender on the butty and spliced some of the worn topstrings. Daphne was still grovelling in the bilges of the motor. Couplings on the shaft had to be inspected as the bolts often worked loose and needed to be tightened or replaced. Unfortunately nuts and bolts, like the windlasses, were almost impossible to replace in those days when all metal was being commandeered for more lethal purposes and, if any of the nuts or bolts were missing, it was necessary to grovel in the bilges until they were retrieved. If a coupling came loose when the boat was in motion, the thrashing and the banging of the disjointed shaft left one in no doubt of the cause! Finally – although not finally at all there was the stern gland to be inspected. The heavy coalbox under the motor counter had to be dragged out – why had we filled it so full? – and the wooden boards of the cabin floor lifted out, leaving just an inch or so at each side of the aperture on which to kneel – or often to lie – in order to check the rest of the shafting. The grease cap had to be unscrewed and the cavity rammed full of the thick yellow grease and the cap lightly replaced. Ideally the cap needed a turn each day to press more grease onto the shaft but it was an additional job which was often ignored or overlooked in the excessive demands of the day's work. Then there was the stern gland, the aperture where the shaft passed through the stern of the hull to the propeller, which had to be packed with lengths of yellow tow to prevent water from the Cut leaking through to the ever-vulnerable bilge.

At last it was all done and I went for a walk along the lay-by, leaving Daphne to a well earned clean-up in the privacy of the cabin. We had seen another pair of the boats crewed by women but the cabins had been padlocked and the crew were on leave. Now, as I passed, there was a trail of smoke from the butty chimney, and the hatch cover was partly open. 'Anyone aboard?' I called.

Cicely peered out and invited me in. She was a New Zealander working her way on a world tour. I was curious to hear how Elsie had survived her trip on the working boats. Cicely assured me that she had done fine. She had worked on the butty the whole of the trip as Susan preferred to take the motor. I had the impression – later to be confirmed – that Cicely was not entirely happy about Susan's preference for the motor. She asked me how I made out on the training boats. I told her I got on fine with Daphne but found the work tedious with new trainees all the time and I told her briefly of our last disastrous trip with Rosalie and Josephine. Cicely had trained with Kit, and she said that Kit wouldn't have put up with them after the first day! I confessed that I'd like to crew on proper working boats, as the last trip with Daphne had been such a pleasant change from all the adversities on the training boats. Cicely was a great decision-taker and said I should join her and Susan, and Elsie could take my place with Daphne. It was with some difficulty that I persuaded her to say nothing; the time was not yet right. We had a couple of new recruits about to join and we had orders to load again at Brentford; Susan and Elsie would not return until the evening and there would be no time for a change of plans. Cicely said we'd keep in touch through the grapevine and I felt cheered at the possibility of change from the tedium of mishaps and hesitant progress on the training boats. I said nothing to Daphne, and when we joined Cicely for 'coffee' our talk was mostly of the ice-up and the other trainees. Elsie had gone to stay with her brother's family in Barnet; the 'Dresden china sisters' had left the boats before Christmas – they had just tied up the boats at Longford, told Mr Vieter and left! Daphne asked if she had heard anything of Margery but all Cicely knew was that Margery had a very efficient crew – we were left wondering!

We were joined the next morning by Pat and Elaine. Pat was hefty and cheerful but also very nervous as we introduced ourselves. Her hands fidgeted and there was an anxious, apprehensive look behind the friendliness of her eyes. More problems, I wondered. Elaine remains but a vague shadow in my memory, reduced to a few lines in my diary: *'One of the new girls has been rejected by Kit and described by her as stupid. Not true but I think that she is physically too weak for the work. She's keen, and Daphne offered to give her a second chance.'* I think she left without completing her first trip. Pat stayed the course despite stomach cramps and sickness. She was pregnant, we discovered much later!

It was well into February. The weather, which so crucially affected our working conditions, was still cold and miserable. There were frosts at night although not hard enough to ice over the canal. The sun had vanished entirely behind heavy mists so that the bright, glittering days of the ice-up seemed preferable by contrast.

Two more trainees, I thought, and neither looked very promising! Being a trainer on the boats was a thankless task; being a trainer's mate even worse, and I began to think more positively about Cicely's suggestion that I join her and Susan. I knew that Elsie would welcome the chance to work again with Daphne. With my own increasing expertise and confidence, it was becoming increasingly irritating to stand by and watch, correct and try to forestall the mistakes and incompetence of the newcomers. It made the work doubly hard when ropes were fouled, when boats were badly steered and when misjudgements of speed and distance incurred laborious and heavy efforts to right them again. Always, it seemed, in our worst predicaments other boats appeared on the scene either to sympathize or to deride, seldom to help. I thought nostalgically of the comparative ease with which Daphne and I had worked the boats two-handed from the coalfield, when the use of the towing line had been such a success. Now we were back to the frustrations of delays and the tedium of explanations and corrections. As a teacher I should have been well suited to the role of instructor, but temperamentally I had never been suited to the irksome, repetitive element of the work – and I had come on the boats to escape from teaching!

My feelings of irritability on the training boats were exacerbated by another of those unfortunate 'incidents'. It happened at Casey (Cassiobury Park) Bridge lock, which is just a nice, ordinary uphill lock as we came from Brentford, glad to be in the countryside after the long suburban stretches through Berker and Ricky. The boats were safely into the lock; Pat and Elaine had wound up the paddles under instruction. I was filling the water cans and Daphne was talking to Pat on the far side of the lock. For the crucial minute no one's attention was focused on the boats. I returned with the water cans to put them on the cabin tops while they were still on a level with the lockside and saw, with horror, that the butty well-deck was full of water. As I read again that diary entry for 11 February I feel once more the shock of seeing the boat gradually submerge under the in-flow of water. To lose a boat in a lock was a recurring nightmare. Not only would the boat have to be salvaged, pumped out and dried, but the ignominy of such negligence would never be outlived. The entry continues the seemingly endless catalogue of incidents and near-disasters aboard the training boats.

11 February
The butty 'ellum was caught under the gate. The stern already was full of water and was sinking rapidly as the lock continued to fill. Frantically we dropped the paddles and rushed to lift the others to let the water out. Never have I raised paddles so fast – and we were only just in time. We baled and baled until the butty floated again above the water. By an absolute miracle the cabin doors were shut. Elaine had put the tiller on the cabin roof instead of propping it in the open hatchway, and the doors had closed with the inrush of water. Even so, there were twelve inches or more of water in the cabin. It was dreadful; everything in the drawers and side-lockers was soaked. We spent a miserable evening with a soggy floor and a damp atmosphere which pervades everything.

Tonight is little better. We're tied at Dudswell and I trailed up to the Cowroast (pub) hoping for a bath. It's a murky night with wind and rain and the towpath is dark and muddy. Of course there was no hot water and no bath; no alternative but to crawl back down that filthy towpath.

It was essential to keep the boats under surveillance every second when locking and to check on every procedure performed by the newcomers until we felt that they too were aware of the possible dangers of mishandling and negligence. Daphne had tried to stagger the newcomers so that one of them was on her second trip, the other a complete novice, but as so many left during their first trip and as the recruitment was so sporadic, it was seldom possible to put theory into practice. Elaine left us somewhere on the way to Tyseley, and it was arranged that Helen join us at Coventry for the return trip. She would have to share the motor cabin with Pat, and again I wondered about the mix of personalities. As it happened, they adjusted well together; they came from similar backgrounds so that habits and conventions related to living in that confined space made it possible for both of them.

'How are Pat's stomach cramps?' I asked Helen.

'Occasional twinges,' she told me. 'She says it's rheumatism, and I thought no more about it. Pat was sensible and took her share of the work so that none of us guessed there was anything seriously amiss. The trip southwards went smoothly, restoring morale and convincing me that canals really were 'my scene'.

For once harmony pervaded the training boats and I began to regret my decision to leave Capricorn and Cleopatra. Then Helen asked me when I intended to have my boats as she was not keen to work as a casual crew member with other trainees whom she would not necessarily know; she would prefer to be one of a more permanent crew. Had I asked Daphne? I confessed I had not and that I felt the need to go as crew on working boats before I would be confident enough to have my own pair.

'It's difficult,' I tried to explain. 'It would be like deserting. It all gets so personal.' I can imagine Helen's acerbic response to my excuses! I said that I would ask Daphne at the end of the trip.

It so happened that we did not return to the depot. We offloaded at Croxley and received orders to return with empty boats to Hawkesbury. There were no new trainees so that Helen and Pat stayed with us. Helen's cryptic comments had needled me out of my passive acceptance of the present ease on the training boats and I began to look for excuses to bolster up my decision to leave.

Then Daphne and I had an argument over lunch one day when we must have been waiting to be loaded. I read from my diary that we disagreed about our relationships with the new recruits. Daphne said that we should 'look after them' and I said that, as they were adults, they should look after themselves – all very stupid and petty!

There is no mention of Pat, so she must have taken leave for a few days while we waited for loading. In fact, she had not been at all well – hardly surprising – but at the time we had no idea of the cause. She did not return to the boats until after the baby was born and then only for a very short while. We were joined by yet another inadequate aspirant to join our small company of boat-women. The only reference to her is in the following brief entry:

4 March
The boats are tied at the top of Nashes ready for unloading. We made a fly trip down from Coventry in four days. Very hard going – terrific winds which once or twice threatened to capsize the boats. We have another new girl in place of Pat. She isn't strong enough for the job. Doing one's own work, helping her, being yelled at by Daphne, listening to complaints from Helen is all too much. I don't think I can bear these training boats much longer.

I knew that the time had come to make a move, and that evening, without preamble or excuse, I said I needed a change and that Cicely and Susan B. had asked me to join them on Bognor and Dodona. It all happened so quickly. Back at the depot I wrote, *'Everyone seems to have congregated. Margery, Jo, Virginia, Cicely, Susan, Olga, Elsie and Kay and many of the others. We had a grand conference. It has been decided that I will do one trip with Susan B. and Cicely. Olga and Elsie said they would like to go on the training boats with Daphne and they have left already.'*

I watched them leave with mixed feelings of regret for the loss of the familiar routine and Daphne's warm companionship and with feelings of apprehension at thought of living and working with two other women of whom I knew little or nothing.

9.   Working Boats

Boats – Bognor and Dodona
Crew – Susan B., Cicely, Margaret
      Susan B., Susan Woolfitt, Margaret

Susan B., who was steerer of the two boats Bognor and Dodona, decided we would wait at the depot for another day on the chance of getting orders to load at the docks. It seemed such an extravagant waste of fuel and manpower to return with empty boats to the coalfields, although, with the docks in increasing disarray from the bombing, this was becoming the rule rather than the exception. Two more pairs crewed by women arrived during the day.

Congregated at the depot there were rumours, and the rumours circulated.

You know that Jo? Wasn't she with you and Daphne? Have you heard? She's queer . . . Asking the trainees to marry her . . . What do you know – is she queer? Why did Daphne let her stay? The woman's a menace . . .

I tried to evade the questions. I had been away with my sprained ligament most of the time Jo had been on the training boats, I said. It was obvious that Jo's affections had not been confined to Daphne and myself. How could she have been so stupid? Margery was on leave and her boats were padlocked, so that the women were left to speculate among themselves. I began to think that Daphne should do something about Jo – she *was* a menace if she could not keep quiet and confine her energies to working the boats. I wondered about Virginia, and someone said she thought Virginia had left the boats. I felt a lurch of disappointment but decided to phone her home later to know of her plans; perhaps she had need to 'escape' from Jo!

I was spared further interrogation as Susan B. decided we should get going and return to Hawkesbury with the empty boats. Spring was in the air, and it was better to be travelling than idling around on the offchance of orders for loading. It would be an easy trip for my first on proper working boats. There was even a feeling of leisure on that trip northwards: '*12 March. It has been so much warmer and the feel of spring is wonderful. . . . There are great bushes of yellow palm and green-yellow catkins, violets and primroses in the grass. . . .*'

After the rigours of the training boats, this trip was much easier and really enjoyable: '*Although we keep going for much longer hours, the work is so much easier when each person knows her job and can be relied upon to do it properly.*'

I was sharing the butty cabin with Cicely (*see* Pl. 13), and we got on well together, at least for the first part of the trip. She was a stimulating yet tiring companion with a great appetite for meeting new people. She was off, she told me, at the end of the trip. She was very irritated with and intolerant of Susan, who was so totally different from herself. Susan was very Irish and a delightful companion, romantic and vague but always ready to do more than her share of the work. It was her privilege as steerer to claim the motor cabin for herself, and she had turned it into a miniature home decorated with lace plates, brass bowls and ornaments which she bought cheaply and then restored with endless sessions of polishing. From her 'home' she spent long hours of steering while Cicely and I lazed away on the butty. She was adept at making tea for herself from the copper kettle she kept brewing on the stove. When she concentrated on the work, there was none better than Susan. Unfortunately she had an 'artistic eye': she was fascinated by the shapes of gates and bridges and would be lost in her own euphoric wonder at the beauty of them while the motor took its own course across the Cut and into the nearest bank. She would turn to point out the 'dear little gate' to the philistines on the butty and be mildly surprised at our shoutings and raised fists. I also think that, with her self-imposed schedule of steering for such long hours without a break or a change, there were bound to be lapses of concentration.

After one such incident Susan rammed the motor so hard that one of the couplings was broken. No doubt the boat had hit a rock but, even so, we felt it was unforgivable. Cicely and I were so annoyed with Susan that we took ourselves off to Leighton Buzzard to do some shopping without even asking her if there was anything she needed. We had tea there and went to the cinema: *'Saw an awful film about a harvest moon. Hitched back to find that Susan had cooked us all a wonderful meal. Coals of fire on our heads!'* How was it possible to resist such penitence? We laughed often at our idiocies of behaviour and at the predicaments in which we so often found ourselves.

We deluded ourselves that our efforts and exertions to transport a few tons of coal or iron pilings or whatever were essential to the nation's defences against invasion. *Did* we delude ourselves? I think that most of us, even Helen, who through her husband must have been aware more than most of us of the threat of invasion, never thought of the work in those terms. The war was a holocaust 'out there', concerned with forces of destruction in which we were in no way involved and yet which had provided this chink of opportunity, this narrow slice of experience, as a kind of by-product of the general mobilization of manpower into armies of uniformed self-righteousness. We were dredged out like small fry from some great net-sweeping operation and we wore self-made haloes as incentives for our unrewarded labours and self-imposed ostracism.

I met with friends on leave from the Services. One was an officer in the WAAF, immaculate and imposing in her tailored uniform, with a batwoman to do the necessary laundering and pressing. I found it hard to reconcile this paragon with the scruffy urchin friend who had tramped the Welsh mountains with me and slept rough on our tours of Dorset and the Loire valley. Another friend, resplendent in her Land Army green and brown, came with tales of handcut rashers from a home-grown pig, of eggs (in the plural!) and of butter churned from the cream of the milk. When she saw our plight and the greed in my eyes, she made a special journey to bring us eggs and butter and a whole pack of pigs' rashers. Her employer, a Wiltshire farmer, had been affected by her tales – dramatized, I feel certain, knowing her gifts in this direction – and had insisted she return laden with his bounty. I think she managed to contact us when we returned to Bull's Bridge, just before Cicely left, as I remember she took charge of the cooking while I took my friend round the lay-by and the workshops. The intoxicating smell of sizzling rashers met me on our return to the Dodona. Irritations and disagreements were forgotten as we ate almost a kilo of the thickly cut rashers at one sitting and mopped up every last globule of fat with our hunks of bread. Ulcers were unheard-of!

I was still accident-prone and, on that first trip with Susan and Cicely, for some unknown reason I stepped off the top planks and landed on my back in the hold of the empty boat. It was the end of a day when, no doubt, I was tired and – like Susan! – I was thinking of something else. I was winded and unable to move for several minutes. Shock was succeeded by panic at being dis-covered. How could I have been so stupid yet again! Slowly and painfully I turned over, flexed arms and legs and tried to stand. Nothing seemed broken although the base of my spine hurt when I moved. Still very shaken, I managed to crawl back to the cabin.

It was impossible to escape from the scrutiny of those sharp, observant eyes and I had to confess what had happened. 'A moment's dizziness,' I excused myself. 'Hungry and tired, I guess.' She was kindness itself and ordered me to bed. Apologies fell out of me like lemmings over the cliff when Susan came around in the morning but their only concern was that I had done no serious damage to my back. At Coventry, Susan came with me to see a doctor, who sent me off for an X-ray and said that it wouldn't be serious as I had been able to walk! I should rest as much as possible!

The damage must have been bruising as I didn't take his advice to rest very seriously. Susan and I hitched to Stratford-on-Avon to see *The Merry Wives of Windsor* and I bought a brass bowl. I did bending and stretching exercises to prevent stiffening, and Susan reported that blues and greens were the colourful indications that the bruise was coming outwards – a good sign!

On the Monday Cicely returned from the four days' leave she had taken while we were waiting to be loaded at Newdigate. We took on beans for Glaxo and then headed southwards once again.

This life was much easier than that of the training boats, and with far more leisure time.

20 March
Tied at the Cowroast last evening. The three of us took a bus into Berker for baths and then to the King's Arms for dinner – such a dinner! Chicken, stuffing, bread sauce etc, etc and two ice-creams each followed by the most perfect coffee. Feeling intoxicated with such good food we retired to the lounge, commandeered three superb armchairs by an open fire and buried ourselves with a pile of magazines for the rest of the evening. The anti-climax came when we missed the last bus back and had to walk the 3½ miles with my back nearly breaking.

We caught up with Daphne at Buckby where both pairs tied at the top of the locks. It would be easier to work the four boats down between us all. Olga was a flamboyant person with colourful trousers and a Mexican-type hat. She shared the butty cabin with Daphne, while Elsie enjoyed the motor cabin to herself. She was enjoying the work but was worried about her brother and his family: the wife wasn't at all well and with three young children was finding it hard to manage as Elsie's brother could seldom get home. She thought she might have to leave the boats to go and help out.

Later, over drinks at the New Inn, where we had bought some of Lord Woolton's infamous pies, I managed to get Daphne on her own to ask if she had any news of Jo. She too had heard the rumours and had been asked by several of the boatwomen that Jo should not be allowed to stay on the boats. She had also heard that there had been a row and that Virginia had left. Memories of Jo's rages made me cowardly thankful that it was Daphne who would have to confront Jo with such a decision and that I would not be around.

We were off the next morning before Capricorn and Cleopatra. Daphne waved us off. 'See you at the depot,' she called. At the office we were told there was a load of aluminium bars if we were interested (*see* Pl. 1). It would only be half a trip as they were destined for Maffas (Marsworth). Cicely said she would stay on for the short trip. She was busy making herself a couple of shirts (by hand!) and decided she would be able to finish them during the few days it would take.

Kit's boats also were at the depot and we met up with another Susan who had completed her training trips and for the past 2½ months had been working with Kit as trainer's mate. Like me, she felt she needed a change from the training boats, and it was agreed that she would join Susan B. and myself when Cicely left. We would wait for her at Southall after we had delivered the bars. She reminded me that she had met Daphne and me back in September after I had hurt my knee. She had come down to Southall to view the boats and to get some idea of what was involved in the work she had blindly – like so many of us – applied to do. She had children at boarding school and could work on the boats only during term time. I listened and watched her surreptitiously – she would be my new cabinmate. She was a great talker!

And then we were off to load with the aluminium bars. I decided that when we next met up with Daphne I would ask her about having my own boats. I had received a letter from Helen asking when she should come. After this half-trip and another with the two Susans I would be ready. Daphne's boats were at the depot when we returned from loading the next day and we had tea with her in Cleopatra. Elsie had gone off to see her brother's family, and Daphne thought it likely she would not return. Olga was away for the day but would be returning that evening. Daphne was waiting for Margery and Jo, as their boats were due in at any time. Susan decided we would stay the night and set off early the next morning. I'd told her I wanted to talk to Daphne about having my own boats after the next trip: I think she and Cicely were also curious to see Jo, having heard of the rumours.

Daphne agreed at once that I should have my own pair and that it would be a good idea if Helen and Virginia would come as crew. She gave me Virginia's home address so that I could phone to find out if she was still willing to come. She told me she'd talked to Miss Minn about the difficulties Jo was creating for herself, and both had come to the conclusion that Jo must be asked to leave the boats. An official letter from the MOT was sent to Jo but it was left to Daphne to ensure that Jo received the letter and complied with the order to leave. I commiserated with her; we both remembered the wild accusations and the rages, and I knew that Daphne was apprehensive about the confrontation. She left the boats early that evening to visit cousins in London and I did not see her again as we left early the next morning for Maffas before she returned.

I did not hear the results of the confrontation until I met up with Daphne some time later. There had been fearful scenes, she told me, and Jo had refused to leave until threatened at the office by police action. That evening she had waylaid Daphne and attacked her. 'I think she might have strangled me,' said Daphne, still shaken by the memory. 'Luckily Olga heard the commotion and came to my rescue.' Later we heard that Jo would appear on the towpath and try to join the boats as they travelled, but, having heard of the scenes back at the depot, everyone was wary of her and she was further warned to keep away. Soon she too disappeared into her own unknown future.

Margery and Jo were not back at the depot by the time we left the following morning so that Susan's and Cicely's curiosity had to be satisfied with my vague and unsatisfactory answers to their questions. When we arrived at the wharf to unload the bars, there was a shortage of men and I offered to put the slings around the bars for the crane-driver as we were anxious not to be held up for too long. Cicely was sorting and packing and Susan was busy in the engine-room. I read in my diary that, much to my surprise, I was paid the princely sum of 4s 10d for 3½ hours work . . . it was welcome as I was almost always broke! Many of the women enjoyed the luxury of independent incomes to supplement the weekly wage of £3. There were others, like myself, who stretched that meagre income to cover food, clothes and such luxuries as baths, cinema and theatre visits when possible. I was also paying 10 shillings a week for my room in Chelsea. It wasn't until years later, when questions arose about pension contributions, that I was envious of my more provident friends who had joined the recognized forces and whose pension rights had been safeguarded during their period of service. Was the experience of working on the boats worth the financial forfeiture? When asked recently if, with hindsight, I would do the same again, I could only reply that I would indeed, despite the difficulties and deprivations.

Cicely bequeathed to me two very welcome sheepskin jerkins. They were sleeveless and laced at the sides, windproof and yet allowing freedom of movement. She also gave me her precious windlass as a 'spare' and a couple of saucepans. She was anxious to be off, beckoned by the next leg of her global adventure. I was both sorry and relieved to see her go – sorry because she was so efficient and easy to live with, but relieved because of her constant irritation with the inoffensive Susan so that I continually found myself in the role of mediator between the two. I thought I too might get more annoyed with Susan's non-organizational way of running the boats and decided to tackle her about the steering before the other Susan should arrive. I suggested we all take turns at steering the motor as this might lessen the possibility of incidents due to lack of concentration. She seemed mildly surprised and said that, as steerer, she thought it was her responsibility to take the motor. I insisted that on the other boats most of the women did take turns. I also added that expertise was soon diminished without practice and that it was only fair that each of us take turns at all the work.

'Most of the trainees don't like the motor,' she protested. Charming as she was, Susan could be very determined.

I told her then that I'd be crewing with her for only one more trip as then I hoped to have my own pair with Helen and Virginia as crew. I suppose I was equally determined as she capitulated and said we'd do a day each on Bognor but that the newcomer would continue to stay on the butty. I still wasn't satisfied but decided that the other Susan would have to fight her own battles; it was possible that, like Elsie and Elaine and Sandra, she'd prefer the butty work. I would only be doing another trip with her and I was beginning to have my own ideas about the best way to run a pair of working boats.

The 'new' Susan was Susan Woolfitt and quite as determined a lady as Susan B. That first evening I told her about Susan's predilection for the motor and of my own confrontation with her. Susan W. temporized and admitted that she preferred the butty work but said that on principle she would insist on taking her share of steering the motor. Kit had said . . . and Kit's word was law to Susan even as Daphne's word had always been for Elsie. We also thought that with two Susans confusions could arise, so when we talked it all over with Susan B., she agreed to be called Bee; we could hardly shorten the Woolfitt to a 'W'!

Susan was the wife of Donald Woolfitt, the well-known Shakespearian actor. She was lively, restless and intelligent, with a fund of fascinating tales of the theatre and great names of the day. As a raconteur she was unique, and her gift must be obvious to all who have read her book *Idle Women*, which she wrote soon after leaving the boats. She was full of enthusiasm and energy and I found her a delightful cabinmate. Whenever she heard that Kit was within cycling distance, she would lift Bee's bike from its cherished place under the cratch and make her perilous way through and round the potholes and the mud to spend an hour or so with Kit and her crew. It was a dreadful old bike and was exposed for riding only when absolutely necessary. We could never tighten the saddle into a rigid position; in fact, it was easier to ride without using the saddle at all. Susan W. managed that bike far better than any of us and it obviously responded to her high opinion of it. After Kit's bike, she said, it was easy! She would ride off down the towpath with no trouble. She said there was a knack to it; maybe, but I never discovered the secret of keeping it steady and preferred to walk – or run – rather than try to cope with its eccentricities.

Between us we managed fairly successfully to organize the unsuspecting Bee so that the trip went smoothly for us all. Brentford docks were still operational and we were loaded again with aluminium bars for Maffas and had orders to continue to the coalfields with empty boats when the bars were offloaded. The spring sun warmed our backs as we steered, and it was so much easier to work through the locks without the encumbrance of jackets and oilskins.

After Blisworth tunnel I took over the motor while Bee took a well-earned rest and made tea for us both down in her cabin. Stowe Hill and the Globe were a favourite stopover, and Bee decided we would tie up there although it was still light. As I idled on the Bognor waiting for the butty to come up on the inside, I saw a pair of boats appear on the stretch through the bridge. I called to Bee that they would have made the Buckby locks ready and that we should carry on to be first up the locks in the morning. She wasn't too keen and said that probably there was a pair ahead of us.

'What about asking?' I said.

They approached – a pair of Joshers owned by Fellows, Morton & Clayton – and we didn't recognize the crew. I called out to ask if the locks were ready for us but no one answered; probably they were in the habit of ignoring 'them women trainees who didn't know what they were about'. They passed us and drew up in the bridge'ole, and it became obvious that they were also stopping but on the other side of the bridge.

'Let's go on,' I said to Bee as she came along the bank to take a rope. Susan also agreed that we should continue as she didn't much care for the look of a couple of mongrel dogs which had come sniffing around the butty. I said I would stay on the motor – I had been enjoying myself.

There were hazards in travelling that stretch as the light faded. The canal winds a furtive passage between high hedges and rough woodland. Outgrowing branches were – and still are at the time of writing – all too ready to sweep cans, mops, windlasses, even bicycles and chimneys from cabin tops as the boats passed underneath. There were sudden narrows where old footbridges had once spanned the water; there were shallows of mud on the offside of bridge'oles as well as on the inside. There was one wide, innocent-looking bend on which the pile-up of mud had silted up both sides so that the channel deceptively and unexpectedly took a middle road round the sweep of the bend. It was to prove my undoing. Either I had forgotten the treachery of this particular bend or I didn't recognize it in the growing darkness. We had been travelling for nine or ten hours and, although I hadn't felt especially tired when we left the Globe, I was beginning to relish the thought of supper and bed. It was darker under the trees than in the open stretch before we reached the Spinneys. 'Never tie up under the Spinneys' was an old saw I had heard from one of the boatpeople and I began to appreciate that it would be less intimidating to travel those dark and wooded bends in daylight than at the end of a tiring day. No doubt my judgement was affected by tiredness and I stemmed up both boats well and truly in the shallows of the 'false' bend under the overhanging trees.

I was deflated, suddenly overtaken by the tiredness which had been threatening, and I was all for leaving the boats where they were as it was unlikely that any other boats would be passing. The others wouldn't hear of it – *I* bloody well had got the boats stemmed up, *I* could bloody well get them off again! Tempers were quickly frayed when working to the point of exhaustion, and I knew that my lack of judgement at the end of a long day was unforgivable. If only we had stayed at the Globe! If only I had let Bee take the motor as I knew she would have preferred! I felt so guilty at prolonging the working day by yet another hour. I tried every trick I knew to free the boats from the oozing mud of that shallow bend but the whole situation was too much for me and I gave up.

The other two reluctantly emerged from the butty cabin where they had been having supper; they had no intention of spending the night there under the Spinneys as they too had heard the old saw. A large owl, white in the darkness, swept down and along the canal with wide wingbeats, and that was enough to fan our feelings of panic. The darkness of the oncoming night seemed to thicken around us so that, from where I stood, the butty was just a darker blur in the darkness and Bee only faintly discernible in the darkness. The beam of the motor's headlight fetched up short against the blackness of the trees; the butty's headlight wasn't working and the faint light from the motor cabin merely made the shadows seem more ghostly and the darkness more impenetrable.

I drank some scalding, gritty cocoa while I waited for them to come and help.

Bee took over the motor and helped me shaft it free, then told me to go back to the butty. There was no one better than Bee in an emergency and I obeyed her orders without question. I crawled under the tiller and grabbed at the higher sides of the butty's bows. I was dragged by Susan onto the foredeck as the motor stern slid from under my feet; but for Susan's heave I would have been yet another casualty! If the RAF had 'gremlins', we had hobgoblins!

Finally the boats were lined up to continue the journey to Buckby. All three of us were unnerved and exhausted so that a moorhen's squawk got us all jumping. I felt absolutely servile in my apologies to Susan as we got under way. 'Shut up,' she said cheerfully. 'Could happen to anyone.'

It's a short stretch from the bend to the tie-up and we arrived dirty, tired and hungry to find boats already there, so that all our hopes of being first for the locks in the morning were quickly dashed. Not that we cared; we were thankful for a helping hand to catch our ropes and to make fast behind the friendly shapes of the pair ahead.

'No good travelling at night,' said Eli from the towpath. 'Specially on that stretch.'

I tried to explain and said that we had seen blind Polly at Stowe who said we'd have the locks if we went on; she probably thought the Nixons would have gone up through. Then there were the Joshers, I said.

Eli agreed that the Joshers were a rough lot but added that they never reckoned to go at night – that they couldn't see the kids.

The barking of dogs and the voices of children on towpath made us feel secure and cheerful again after the black gloom under the trees only half a mile back down the Cut. After a quick wash and another snack we decided to go to the pub; it was almost deserted and we told our tale to the amused barman.

'You were right not to spend the night under the trees,' he told us. 'None of the boatmen ever reckons to tie up under the Spinneys – they say it's a bad place after dark.' He could tell us nothing more.

In daylight the Spinneys was – and is – a delightful stretch with a broad towpath and fields on one side and a tangle of trees and bushes on the other, giving welcome shade from the heat on a summer day. Later, when I was working with Virginia and Helen, we met up with Bee and recalled the events of that time I stemmed the boats up under the trees.

'We always go through the Spinneys in daylight,' said Bee.

'Same for us,' I replied and, although we laughed at the memory of our panic, it was tacitly agreed by us all that the Spinneys was to be avoided after dark – whatever the reason. We were boatwomen – if only trainee boatwomen – and we were beginning to inherit the beliefs, customs and superstitions along with the way of life we had adopted.

It seems strange, as I re-read my account of the episode, that we were so scared and impressionable. The Spinneys is now one of my favourite stopping places. There is a boat's length of concrete coping under the trees where I spend many delightful days on the Alphons tied up well away from intrusions of casual callers. It never seems in the least spooky or frightening, even at night. The only possible hazard of mooring there is from falling branches in a high wind and I'm sure that this was the most likely danger to have threatened us as we struggled to escape from some less tangible peril.

144

The next morning we heard sounds of the lock being drawn in the pale chill of an April dawn and knew we'd have an extra hour in bed. It was sensible to let the Nixons get well ahead, and there was always the possibility that another pair might come down the locks, which would save us the extra work of lockwheeling. A wind was beginning to gust the boat against the bank and there was a spatter of rain on the cabin roof. April showers and winds, I thought, but sun as well if we were lucky. My dozing content was sharpened into wakefulness by a bang on the cabin side with the mop.

'Up time,' said Susan breezily but, thankfully, for both of us speech was reduced to monosyllabic grunts in those early mornings; it was at night that we both waxed eloquent, talking far into the night when we might have been sleeping.

12 April
9 a.m. start – such luxury! The Nixons left at 7 a.m. No boats coming down so we had to lockwheel. All has gone well today despite wind and blustery showers. I took the motor through Braunston tunnel with never a scrape – have redeemed myself! Bee has toothache. Tied up early in Braunston so that she could see a dentist. No dentist available. We managed to get some aspirin.

The following day Bee was feeling decidedly unwell and Susan persuaded her to rest in the butty cabin away from the noise of the engine. I was to take the motor. All went well until we came to Shuckburgh corner and there, jammed hard across the bend, was a single coalboat, a Fellows-Morton-&-Clayton. As I approached cautiously, I saw that it was the Python and I knew that the steerer was an old enemy of Daphne's. He had rammed her boats, broken the snubber, put them on the mud and almost knocked Daphne into the Cut. This all happened before I joined the boats but Daphne had warned me that he was no friend to us women trainees – one of the very few antagonists, I'm thankful to say. What should I do? I looked back at Susan but she only shrugged; I would have to make my own decision. We could stop and wait until he shafted his way out of the bend or we could try to edge our boats past him, though, as he had stuck, we might well do the same and incur his rage at my stupidity. There was no sign of the man; to save face he had strategically disappeared until he could see who was on the approaching boats. As we were only 'them women trainees', he might well have stayed hidden until dark, and in any case we would have to stop the boats in the channel as there was no chance of reaching the banks on the muddy approach to the bend.

I decided to take the risk and to edge the Bognor around as near as I dared to the Python. I signalled to Susan that I would go ahead, made a quick prayer-sign with my hands and turned to concentrate. There was still no movement aboard the Python but I knew that every move would be watched. The Bognor was a good boat and responded well to a judicious flick of the tiller even when throttled down. 'Help me not to stick,' I prayed fervently as I edged the boat round the bend as near as I dared to Python without touching. The blades were turning with barely a ripple – 'Please don't let the engine cut' – and then I was past. I gathered in the length of towing line which had become slack as the butty came following up behind; luckily it had not been drawn under round the prop. Susan was rowing hard on the tiller to keep a good distance between Dodona and Python. There was no sign of Bee so she must have been dozing and only half aware of the risk I had taken with her precious boat.

Now to manœuvre the butty without grazing the new paint of Python. There was still no sign of the steerer although, from the tail of an eye, I thought I saw one of the engine-room doors open just a fraction. I was too intent on getting our boats round to look more closely. I made a quick stop, shortened the towing line as much as possible and then went hard ahead to pull the bows of Dodona away from the Python. The wash would push his boat further over but, as the bows were firmly embedded in the bank, I thought he could hardly complain. Twice I had to straighten up and repeat the operation before the butty finally came clear. I was so elated by my success that I shouted to Susan that I would offer to give Python a snatch, and I loosed off the butty to let it drift on its way. Susan shook her head and waved her hands in a negative gesture and Bee, who had emerged to see what all the commotion was about, shouted 'No' at me and to carry on.

I was too inflated with my success to listen. I took the Bognor astern – she steered well in reverse, unlike some of the boats – while the Dodona slid past with Susan and Bee still shouting at

me. The steerer of Python had now emerged from the engine-
room.

'Something wrong with the engine,' was always a face-saving
excuse to cover a mistake.

'Can I give you a snatch?' I shouted cheerfully.

He was gracious enough to accept my offer and threw me a line
from the bows. With a few bursts from the Bognor's engine the
Python soon came free.

'Got too much on,' he said by way of thanks. It was enough. I
threw back his line, waved and caught up with the butty. I knew
we had 'scored' as he deliberately held back while I picked up the
butty and went ahead. He could have passed us easily with a
single motor. In fact, he turned southwards at Napton Junction
while we turned under the bridge for Tyseley.

When I had my 'own' boats on the Oxford run we met with
Python quite frequently, and I was always ready with my 'How
do' but the unresponsive slouch of the steerer behind the
chimney soon halted the greeting in my throat and I too learned
to slouch behind the protection of the chimney as if he didn't
exist!

'You took a chance there,' said Bee later. 'He'd have scalped
you if you'd stuck as well.'

'Panic got the adrenalin flowing – otherwise I might not have
made it,' I admitted.

Susan commented that it was a pity the adrenalin hadn't
flowed when I had stemmed the boats up under the Spinneys!

At Tyseley we heard rumours and trickles of news that the
Allies had advanced into Germany and that the end of that
endless war was in sight. I owned a portable Pie radio which at
the time seemed the height of luxury. Unfortunately there were
no such refinements as transistors and micro-chips, and the dry
battery would work only with an accumulator which had to be
charged every few days to make the set operable – an impractical
arrangement for our nomadic way of life. Now, I wonder why we
did not have a trickle charger but, like many other women of my
generation, the mysteries of chemistry and physics were not
included in our school curriculum. The only time I remember
wishing for a reliable radio was during that trip round to the
coalfields when the excitement of anticipation was in the air. The
accumulator was nearing the end of its temporary charge; Susan

and I switched on the set for seconds at a time to hear the latest news. Then the sound would start to fade and we turned it off immediately to save the precious juice in the hope that we might catch the gist of a more newsworthy bulletin. But in the end we did hear the announcement that the Germans had surrendered:

8 May
News of peace came over the loud speaker at Newdigate where we are coaled. The loaders rushed off. Bee and I were left to level off and to cloth up. It is very hot. We were excited and tried to listen to the bulletins as we worked, so that clothing up was rather a leisurely process. Mr Flowers came along to view the loading of the motor. He wouldn't let us rest until we had shovelled almost a ton off onto the butty.
10 May
Two days' holiday. Bee, Susan and I hitched down to Stratford thinking there would be great rejoicings.

I had wanted to return to London and to dance in the streets with all the exuberance and emotion generated by mass exhilaration and personal relief, but Bee and Susan persuaded me to join them instead. There was little rejoicing in Stratford, only an apprehensive pessimism.

Everything was just dead. We went to the theatre and saw Twelfth Night, *had drinks and then returned to our B & B, an excellent place where we breakfasted on bacon and eggs – all for 6s.6d. Next day we went for a boat trip up the river and then to a performance of* She Stoops to Conquer – *far superior to TN. I don't think much of R. Atkins as an actor.*

With some difficulty Bee and I hitched back to Hawkesbury. Susan had decided to stay on in Stratford with theatre friends and would join us again at Knowle. Bee and I had rather a dreary journey, both of us morose and depressed without Susan's vivacity to rally our dejection. But we cheered on seeing lights blazing everywhere on the boats and in the houses at the Stop. For me, by far the best celebration of the peace was at the Stop, where we joined in the festivities on our return from Stratford. After six years of total black-out at the end of each day, the uninhibited flare of light from windows and doorways was the most heart-warming sign of a return to sanity.

Last evening at Hawkesbury there was a bonfire. We sat and watched the children dancing round and then everyone started to sing. It was 'Pack up your troubles' and 'The Siegfried Line' and 'We'll meet again' with the notes slurred sentimentally into each other. Mr Finch was there with young Sydney, whose energy was boundless. Mr Finch fed us all with ginger wine from a glass used by us all. Mrs Humphries was there with all her children; occasionally she tried to gather up young Ronnie, who insisted on rushing round and round the bonfire, thrilled to death.

After a lifetime of knowing only the exigencies of the black-out, it must have been a wonderful experience for a five-year-old.

In the pram was the five-month-old baby. Directly it awoke it was sat upright by an older sister and it viewed everything with a lively interest. Hilda Humphries, with her leg in splints after a nasty accident in a lock, was nursed by Bee. We finally retreated at 12.30 a.m. – everyone still drinking and dancing.

The next day it was back to normality, and Mr Flowers' concern for our loading was fully justified: *'11 May. An early start. Have found the extra coal a great trial. We sit in every muddy bridge'ole and are taking hours to get anywhere.'*

After a tedious trip, with heavy boats and the water low in the pounds, we finally offloaded at Croxley and then returned to the depot at Bull's Bridge. Susan had decided to leave the boats and I was to take charge of my own pair. I was convinced that I had learned from the experience on the training boats all the technical details of how to work the boats efficiently and, from the experience of working on Bognor and Dodona, how best to keep a crew together.

Margery was at the depot and was clearing out her boats ready to leave. She was grim-faced and uncommunicative when I asked her when, or if, Virginia was likely to return to the boats. No, she didn't know anything of Virginia's plans. Capricorn and Cleopatra were also tied up in the lay-by but there was no sign of Daphne until the following day. She was going to do a trip with

Audrey on working boats as the thin trickle of new recruits had almost ceased. She confirmed that the boats Hercules and Cetus had been overhauled for me if I could get a crew together.

I phoned Helen that evening. Yes, she would come at the end of the week. I left a message with Virginia's young sister that I hoped she would come and join Helen and myself as soon as possible. I didn't feel very hopeful as the sister said Virginia was not staying at home but that she would try to contact her. It so happened that she was staying with Ruth, an old friend of her mother, who was to join us on our last trip on the boats. At the time I was rather depressed by the thought that Virginia might not be there to share in the planning and the running of the boats, and I wondered too who there might be to share the butty cabin with Helen, as I was selfishly determined to retain the privilege of reserving the motor cabin for myself. I wandered down the lay-by and almost wished I had stayed with Bee. She was such a friendly and capable boatwoman that it was only my own ambition to be in charge of a pair which had decided me to work on her boats only as a temporary arrangement. I think that, had she not left with another crew, I would have returned that day to the known comforts of the Dodona's cabin. Audrey and Evelyn were preparing to leave with Daphne aboard, and Margery had only one more day on the boats before she would have left for good. She offered to sell me some of the equipment she had bought for the cabins and, half-heartedly, I agreed to buy, still uncertain who would join Helen and myself as a third crew member if Virginia should not return. I knew there was pressure on her at home to continue at university but hoped that perhaps she might join us for the summer months before term started.

10. *Steerer of a Pair*

Boats – Hercules and Cetus
        Hyperion and Cetus
Crew – Margaret, Virginia, Helen

I looked at the boats, Hercules and Cetus, and wondered however they could be restored to functional and reputable standards of usage. Both boats were half full of water, the sidecloths drooped wretchedly over the sides of the holds and I could see that most of the topstrings were missing. They were tied end-on to the lay-by and I peered into the engine-room doors. I wrote in my diary that the engine-room was in a state of indescribable filth and that I was sure the engine had not been overhauled despite assurances from the office that all the necessary work had been done; events on our first trip out were to confirm my own suspicions that no fitter had as much as looked at the engine. I inspected the cabins and miserably decided that they were almost uninhabitable. However, I hauled along my few possessions and dumped them in the butty cabin, which was the cleaner of the two. I lit the primus I had bought from Margery and decided to cheer myself up with a mug of tea while I decided what I should do first.

I remember sitting there in the untidiness of the cabin when I

151

heard a shout from the bank. It was Virginia and the faithful Candy. Her sister had phoned Ruth and she had left immediately. She had been about to take a secretarial course as she thought I had probably left the boats. There had been an awful row on Margery's boats with Jo, and she had just left and had heard nothing since. I told her what I knew about Jo and assured her that Jo had left the boats. She was pleased to come back to the boats, she said, as the thought of office work dismayed her.

Virginia's return dispelled my despair so that I began to see the possibilities instead of the somewhat daunting realities.

'Let's do the butty cabin so that we have somewhere to sleep,' I said after a further inspection of the boats. 'Helen can't come until the end of the week.'

Optimistically I wrote: *'I think a week's hard work will be necessary to get the boats in to shape.'* But as the week continued we both decided that two could work more efficiently than three, and we grinned at the thought of the immaculate Helen sandpapering those rust-encrusted stoves! I phoned her at intervals to let her know of Virginia's return and of our progress on the boats. It was as well that she hadn't returned as we were not able to tackle the cabin on Hercules until several days later. We managed to clean off the rust from the stove in Cetus and to beg a new chimney from the blacksmith so that we were able to get a good fire going and make the cabin reasonably comfortable. There followed days of endless activity.

30 May
Interviews with blacksmiths, electricians, carpenters, sailmakers and fitters – although there are only two of the latter, both overworked and on boats away from the depot most of the time. We have painted all the top planks, the masts and uprights. We have scrubbed and cleaned up the engine-room, swept and cleaned the filthy holds after baling them out with tins and buckets.

I wonder why there were no handpumps! All the work was done the hard way, with no solvents, no vacuum cleaners or even rubber gloves. At the top of my lists were priorities such as sandpaper, wire brushes, wire wool, scrubbing brushes, buckets, Vim, Brasso and paintbrushes.

As the steerer of a pair I was responsible for equipping both the cabins with the basic necessities for living aboard, and I was thankful to buy from Margery the discarded items from her boats. I see that for £3.2s.3d. I bought two oil stoves, a primus, an axe, a chimney brush, a teapot and a kettle, a washing-up bowl and a paraffin can. I spent a further £4.5s.6d. on such items as buckets, broom, brushes, saucepans and frying-pans, basins, an enamel jug, another kettle, two padlocks and a potato-peeler! There was no allowance made for equipping the cabins, and the cryptic comment that I had just £2 left until we would be paid must have meant a bread-line existence. However, the proud moment when I heard over the tannoy 'Steerer Cornish to report to the office for orders' more than compensated for any feeling of deprivation.

It was a luxury also to have my own cabin despite the fact that it was bug-infested. I woke up on the first morning when finally both cabins had been made habitable, with large red lumps all round my hairline.

'Bugs,' said Vi from boats tied near us. 'Wooden boat. Never get rid of them.'

The cabin was sealed and a sulphur candle was kept burning for forty-eight hours. Every night I used to spray the cracks between the boards with DDT. Vi was right: the bugs were discouraged but they never wholly disappeared.

Helen returned and, as we waited for orders, her talents began to blossom: '*Helen has been painting roses and castles in our cabins and on the door panels. They are the envy of all the boaters, who are trying to persuade her to paint for them as well.*'

During the time I was with Daphne and then with Bee I had plenty of time to think about the best way of working a pair of boats with a crew of three women. Most of the trainees preferred to follow the example of the boatpeople so that the steerer took over the responsibility for steering the motor for most of the time. The steerer on the working boats was almost always the man, so that his mate, usually his wife, would be back in the butty with the younger children and able to do the cooking while the boats were under way. This was the general pattern, although not necessarily so, as the mate would sometimes be another young man looking for a job until he, in turn, might marry and be successful in being employed by the Company as steerer of a pair. When the wife was heavily pregnant or unfit, the steerer would have to depend on these spares to work as his mate. Bee, Margery and many others followed this traditional way of working the boats.

There was a certain advantage in this method: the steerer grew proficient more quickly in the use of the motor and adept at fire-stoking, brewing up and snack-making while still on the move, and the pair on the butty organized the rest of the work between them. But I had begun to watch for Bee's spells of poor concentration and then I'd heard of an incident on Margery's boats – confirmed by Virginia. Margery had twisted an ankle and was forced to let one of her crew take the motor. The poor trainee not only was inexperienced at steering the motor but also had to take the brunt of Margery's caustic comments and advice from her enforced rest in the cabin. I decided that in these conditions the division of labour was preferable and, in the long term, more efficient than specialization. The three of us considered two-hourly shifts the most practical arrangement so that each one in turn would spend two hours steering the motor, two hours steering the butty and two hours 'off', which would entail lock-wheeling, shopping, cooking or cleaning or . . . This we said hopefully, would ensure a degree of variety in the long working day and in our relationships with each other.

As I had optimistically surmised, we were a good crew, although so very different from each other. Helen, at thirty-four, was elegant, practical and blessed with a marvellous sense of humour which often rescued us from total despair on the bad days. We never quite became reconciled to her insistence on wearing gloves at all times so that her hands would not be ruined: we shouted at her and her gloves when she bungled the ropes but she bore us no malice; regrets on both sides cancelled out the temporary rancour! Virginia was the youngest, at twenty-one; she was strong, capable and with the most equable temperament. I was somewhere in the middle in both age and temperament – equable enough on the good days but easily depressed and irritable when everything seemed to go wrong.

Meanwhile, back at the depot, as Virginia and I continued to scrub and to scrape, to splice, to beg-borrow-and-steal odd ends of ropes for fenders and tipcats, to paint and to polish until fingers and hands were sore and blistered, gradually the boats were restored to a reasonable standard of appearance and convenience. I was still suspicious of the engine and I knew that once we left the depot it would be difficult to get a fitter to come and effect any repairs.

I made lists and lists to include such items as shackles and chains, flue brush and spare chimney (if we were lucky!), grease, tow, flex and sandpaper, spanners and screwdrivers, tiller pin, half-inch nuts, wire-cutter, baler tin, sharp knife, paintbrushes, pipe-cleaners, wire, clothes' line, large hammer etc. There was no one to prompt us with, 'Have you remembered . . . ?' It was too bad if we forgot anything in that first frantic week of preparing a pair of boats for a renewal of their working life.

Finally we were as ready as ever we would be. Helen and Virginia were settled, with Candy, into the butty cabin. The stove shone, there was linoleum on the floor, and the table-cupboard was stocked with tins and packets mostly brought by Helen from her home in Wiltshire. I had painted out the cabin in Hercules with cream paint, partly to deter the bugs but also to lighten the gloom – it had been painted in a very dark green. The stove in my cabin was a Nipper range, a smaller version of the Diamond range on the Cetus but efficient enough for cooking and heating. A few books and possessions made it home for me, as my gipsy caravan once had been.

'Steerer Cornish report for orders,' came over the tannoy as I was luxuriating over tea in my cabin. Rather self-consciously I joined the three or four men also waiting for orders in the office.

'Like to work for Sam Barlow on the Oxford?' I was asked. 'Miss Vlasto and crew on Hyperion and Capella are leaving after another trip, and Mr Barlow wants another pair of trainees.' The sceptical tone of voice indicated mistrust of Mr Barlow's judgement. I was sure the other two would be agreeable, I said, and asked when we were to start. Immediately, I was told. We would take the boats empty to the coalfields and the load up for Wolvercote papermills.

Oxford again! I was thrilled at the prospect. I would see again the red buses hurrying up and down the High; we'd be able to go to the Playhouse and browse around the bookshops in Broad Street and perhaps to swim again in the shadowed stretches of the Isis. I thought of my one cursory visit to the canal when I had been living near Iffley lock at the other end of the city. Never a thought had entered my mind that, in a couple of years, I would be travelling with a pair of boats along that muddy stretch.

'Well?' the voice broke irritably through the random images. 'Others waiting,' he reminded me.

'Yes, thanks,' I said hurriedly and escaped.

Virginia and Helen were as delighted as I. We had heard that Sam Barlow was a very considerate employer and that he paid Christian and her crew during leave as well as while they were working! And the Southern Oxford would be an adventure and a change from the old familiar route of the Grand Union.

'Single locks too,' said Virginia.

Little did we realize how we would long for the large double locks and the deep water of the main line!

Full of optimism we sat and talked, made a last check that all was ready for the morning and then turned in to be fresh for an early start.

It was a beautiful day in early June as we swung the engine into action and manœuvred the boats out from the lay-by, conscious that eyes would be watching and assessing our competence. We went singled out, with the butty tied up to the motor stern with the short crossed straps, I doing the first shift on the motor while Virginia and Helen enjoyed the leisurely ride to Cowley lock. It was a wonderful start with the feel of the tiller in my back, the slow throb of the engine and the fresh smell of an early summer day all around me.

Feelings of exhilaration were soon dispelled! As we approached the lock and I throttled down for breasting up, the accelerator cable came loose in my hand and the engine cut out. I headed for the bank, my only form of braking. I saw the lock-keeper opening the gates and shouted to him that the engine had cut. Somehow Virginia managed to get onto the bank and we roped the two boats into the lock. At the top the lock-keeper phoned the depot for us, and despondently we waited a whole day until one of the fitters arrived. He patched up the cable and, as I stood there watching, gave a cursory check to other essentials.

'Hasn't been serviced, has it?' I asked.

'An old boat,' he said with a shrug. 'Get it changed if you have a chance. Working for Mr Barlow, are you? He'll see you right. Phone him when you get to the Stop.'

Meanwhile we had to carry on with the old Hercules, and that first week out my diary reads like a chronicle of disasters.

8 June
. . . Acceleration cable patched up at Cowley but the engine still cuts
out in neutral. I've fought with a blocked fuel pipe – cleared it. All the
bolts came out of two of the couplings which has resulted in a bent shaft
and a wrecked stern gland . . . and a completely wrecked cabin. [So
much for the privilege of the motor cabin to myself!] I found most of the
nuts and bolts in the bilges – no spring washers or locking nuts! Finally
there's an awful leak from the cabin bilge into the engine-room bilge,
causing endless trouble.
12 June
We managed to get to Baddesley to load despite terrific winds which
continuously blow the empty boats on the mud. The butty 'ellum came
off – crawled down Atherstone in rather a miserable state.

The butty 'ellum was often a problem in the narrow locks of the
Coventry and Oxford canals, where the lock chambers were only
just long enough to take the length of the boats. It was in the top
lock of Atherstone that the rudder caught on the cill as the lock
emptied and was lifted upwards and off the two iron sockets into
which the prongs of the 'ellum were slotted. To replace the
rudder required strength, precision and co-ordination between
the three of us to lower the unwieldy bulk so that the prongs – or
pins – could be slotted back into the sockets on the stern of the
boat. A rope was threaded through the tiller slot at the top of the
'ellum so that, by dint of heaving from above and lifting from
below, the great weight was lifted from its muddy resting place
on the cill and guided into position. More often than not, the
operation had to be repeated several times before the two prongs
were completely aligned so that they dropped simultaneously
into the slots. As the back end of the butty curved inwards, it was
a near-impossible manœuvre for the limitations of our strength,
and that first time we did indeed 'crawl down Atherstone in a
miserable manner' with the rudder loosely caught back on its top
pin and then roped as firmly as possible to keep it from further
disaster.

At the bottom of the locks we knew we had to find help, and
luckily Bill Beresford appeared on the towpath. His boats had
been loaded and were approaching the locks. The Hercules was
tied up by the towpath while the three of us had struggled with
the flapping rudder in the empty bottom lock.

'Close bottom gates,' said Bill and we obeyed blindly; he would know what to do. He lifted a paddle to start refilling the lock. When the cill was well covered, he dropped the paddle and told Virginia and me to pull the butty to the back of the lock. He then emptied the lock so that the back end of the butty rested on the cill while the rest of the boat sloped downwards to the bed of the empty lock. I saw at once that the angle of the stern made the slots far more accessible. He told one of us to get down into the lock to guide the rudder as he dropped it. With his man's muscle he swung the rudder easily from where he stood on the gate. Within seconds the rudder was swinging freely again on its pins, the boat was refloated and the lock once more emptied and ready for the oncoming boats. 'Never try that trick with a loaded boat,' he cautioned. 'Could break its back.'

The only other time we lost the rudder was at Hillmorton, again with empty boats. How could we have been so careless? Apprehensively we repeated the manœuvre learnt at Atherstone and succeeded in replacing the rudder, although the weight of it reduced us all to near exhaustion. It was essential to compensate for lack of brawn with better use of brain, I thought, if we were going to survive! Already we were threatened with feelings of discouragement by the continual difficulties of that first trip on the Hercules, and there were times when I really hated that boat! There was one ray of hope that things might improve. I phoned Mr Barlow to complain about the state of the engine. He said he was hiring the boats from the GUCCC and that the company was responsible for their maintenance. I told him how difficult it was to get a fitter and he suggested that on our return trip we call in at Nurser's yard in Braunston and he would ensure that someone would be there to help us. I asked him about the possibility of taking over Hyperion, Christian Vlasto's boat, as I'd heard she was leaving. He agreed immediately and said we would meet up with them at Hawkesbury and to arrange the change-over between us. Only the thought of taking over the Hyperion kept us going through the ensuing disasters.

15 June
Finally loaded with coal for Osberton Radiators. Trouble all the way; we are all very tired. Every day is a struggle to keep going and every day something goes wrong. At Nuneaton Helen got the snubber

round the blades. Tried to hook it off with the shaft for ages. Got into bathing costume and spent an hour hacking it off. Freezing cold – bread knife ruined – our new snubber as well – no hope for another.

The stern gland was again giving trouble. Each night, after a brief wash and a meal, I hoped to relax for an hour before bed with a book. We had 'good' coal on board so there was plenty for our ranges. Although it was June, the weather was cold and uncertain. As I sat, half dozing, the ominous drip started. I tried to ignore it, then tried to gauge the density of the drips and the time between each one, to assess whether or not the bilge would fill during my six or seven hours of sleep. As I tried not to listen, the steady drops grew more insistent and I knew I could not afford to take chances. There was also that leak through the bulkhead to the bilge in the engine-room, and I knew that the alternative to repacking the stern gland would be at least an hour's baling by hand the following morning to reduce the level of the bilge below the reach of the flywheel. I was so tired that only the thought of the next morning and the silent reproval of my mates spurred me on to the necessary action. Wearily I lifted the floorboards and stacked them on the counter, then forced another length of the yellow turd of tow into the aperture between the shaft and its casing. The bent shaft, caused by the loosened couplings, was the source of the trouble and I decide to make use of Mr Barlow's offer and take the boats back into Braunston. There was a dry dock there if the shafting had to be renewed.

Our hopes were soon dashed. There was no one at the yard and when I phoned the depot to complain of our plight I was told to carry on. Bert Tooley at Banbury might be able to help in an emergency. I tried to explain that the loosened couplings had not been our fault (although I began to think that I *should* have checked them before we left) but I felt I was making excuses and that I was just another of those troublesome trainee women to the unsympathetic voice at the other end. It seemed I would have to endure the nightly ritual of packing the stern gland and pray that it would get no worse.

A pair of Joshers was tied up nearby and, as I returned from the yard, I began to complain bitterly about our troubles to the boatman on the towpath. I told him about the leak through the bulkhead.

'Let's have a look,' he said, as I half hoped he might.

Floorboards up again and he lowered himself into the narrow gap.

'Easy to plug that leak into the engine-room,' he said, probing around under the oily recesses of the cabin bilges. 'Seems the bulkhead has rusted through a bit.' He also found that the grease cap on the bearings had rusted solidly – no wonder I had not been able to move it! He chiselled it off, filled the aperture and the cap with scoops of thick yellow grease and then hammered the cap back into position.

'Best I can do,' he said. 'Tell them at the depot to do something about it. Should get you to Radiators all right. Shallow though, the Oxford.'

I wanted to pay him for his trouble and time. It was a delicate matter but I knew that coal was always an acceptable commodity for barter. His boats were sheeted up, which meant they were carrying a more general cargo. We had on a load of good domestic coal and, no doubt, he had noted it. I'm not suggesting that this was the reason for his help but doubtless it weighed in the balance.

'Coal?' I asked.

'Used to have a horse,' he prevaricated. 'Sooner have my National any road . . . We've run out . . . I'll bring a bucket.'

He took out several buckets from the motor hold which he emptied into the bunker at the back end of his butty. 'The missus will be glad,' he commented as we took our leave. I never saw his missus. All such transactions were done by the men; the work on the engine and the exchange of coal between the man and the trainee were classified in the woman's mind as 'man's work and nowt to do with her'.

We decided not to wait for the possible appearance of one of the elusive fitters. The boatman had said we should get there all right and we had such faith in his judgement! We turned the boats in the narrow opening of Nurser's small dock and, optimism once more restored, set off for the unknown reaches of the Southern Oxford. There were no maps available and no instruction sheets; it was like a trip of exploration into uncharted territory. The canal was then – as now – a shallow and twisty waterway with narrow, single locks and, apart from the Skinners and the Humphries with their single, horse-drawn boats, there was little other traffic.

At Shuckburgh we left the top Oxford, keeping south-west for Napton. I wondered if we would meet up again with Python.

16 June
Came through glorious country, past meadows thick with long grass and between banks profuse with innumerable varieties of wild flowers. It remains cold and the rain is everlasting; we all long for some really decent weather. Helen again caught the shortened snubber in the blades just as we started but it freed quite easily with no loss of length. All went well – came to Napton locks – worked the boats up singly. At the top the engine chugged, shuddered and stopped. Have tried everything – the valves, the oil, the intake filter – all I can think of. We are tied in a glorious place, right in the heart of the Cotswolds – but, of course, there's no water! [Drinking water]

Wandered round the fields this evening after finding a phone to report the breakdown to Mr Barlow and to the office. Picked scarlet and pink roses, starry horsedaisies and ragged robins. There were elm trees standing in a frieze against a hill, and a windmill with a broken sail etched on the horizon.
18 June
Still tied at the top of Napton with the engine in pieces on the bank. George from Hatton has arrived and found that several parts of the engine are completely worn out and have to be replaced. I have written to Mr Bridger [of GUCCC] to complain as these boats have been hired to Mr Barlow.

Meanwhile we have had a peaceful time doing all our chores. The Cut water is clean enough for washing and George has brought us drinking water in a churn. Scrubbed my cabin thoroughly with disinfectant – the bugs are active again.

Helen has gone home. Virginia and I discovered a small RAF bombing outpost about two miles off – we have been there all day and eaten endless meals. Sat on the grass with Don and Douglas discussing problems of the demobbed serviceman!

Last evening we walked up to the fair at Priors Marston. One roundabout, two sideshows, two gambling booths in a setting of elm trees and meadows. Had ten minutes on the roundabout for 6d.!

While we were enjoying 'endless meals' at the RAF station, George from Hatton and George from Bull's Bridge worked on the heap of metal assembled on the bank. It was difficult to believe that it could ever be reunited into a working whole.

'You must have sounded pretty fierce on the phone for them to have sent *two* fitters,' said Virginia when the second George arrived. I said that I was learning; the letter to Mr Bridger hadn't been too sweet either!

We sat on the bank as the last chunks of metal were reassembled to complete the great octopus in the engine-room. As we sat there sunning ourselves and enjoying the last hours of our enforced holiday, a horse appeared on the towpath from under the bridge in the distance and then, silently gliding in its wake, came the Friendship, the single boat owned and worked by Rosie and Joe Skinner. Virginia got up to make tea for the workers while I made the lock ready for the oncoming boat. I talked with Rosie and admired their horse, which seemed so dependable compared with the laborious unpredictability of the Hercules' engine. The horse looked so well cared for and knew its work with little or no command from Joe, although Rosie assured me that it had not always been the case. This one – I forget its name – had been with them for six years. Before that they had tried two or three which had been difficult to train and finally had proved unsuitable.

'Get a good horse and there's no further trouble,' she said. 'But a bad 'un leaves you fretted and worn at a day's end.'

I was reminded of the notorious Arthur whose enthusiasm could never be curbed and who tried to do everything at the gallop – with disastrous results!

'How much you got on?' asked Joe as we toiled down the locks.

'Twenty and twenty-five,' I answered.

He shook his head, 'Shouldn't have given you more than eighteen and twenty. Water's low. Have to watch it on the tunnel.'

I watched them glide on their way with something like envy. As I returned up the locks, the sound of the engine greeted me. The two Georges were stowing tools and oily rags into the back of the van.

'Should be all right,' said George-from-Hatton – he was the friendly one. 'We've done the best we can. You're taking Hyperion next trip. You'll have no trouble with that one.'

'We still have to get to Wolvercote and back,' I said, only partly reassured about the competence of the Hercules' engine to complete the trip. 'Joe said we'd got too much on for the Oxford.'

'Know what you can do with the extra,' he said with a wink.

I'd willingly have encouraged him to take as much as he liked of the stuff but George-from-the-depot could well have carried tales to the office and I couldn't take the risk. He had brought a message that we were to offload at Wolvercote papermills instead of Osberton Radiators. 'Where was that?' I asked.

'Just carry on past Radiators,' was the only information I could get from either of them; they seemed to think there was no problem, so I presumed that the mills would become self-evident.

Then they were gone and I was able to replace the floorboards in my cabin and clean up – yet again! – so that the cabin was restored to its feeling of home. I phoned Helen to tell her that Virginia and I would get the boats on their way the next morning, and she said she would meet us at a place called Fenny Compton where the railway ran close to the canal. I was always amazed at the ease with which she found buses and trains to transport her to and from her home whenever her husband was on leave or whenever she found it necessary to restore morale and energy for a further stint on the boats. Virginia and I worked well together but we were always thankful to see the return of Helen's familiar figure on the towpath.

It was late afternoon when we saw her waiting for us from a bridge.

'A man said that something called the tunnel is just ahead and that we should go through at half revs,' she told us as she came aboard. She took over the butty while Virginia steered the motor and I checked the pumps, the oil gauge and the charging meter and then perched on the cabin roof to record the significant features of our journey down the Oxford. We came to the 'tunnel' which we now know is just a narrow cutting between the high banks. We slid along that muddy ditch with the blades just turning to keep the boats moving. Virginia rowed with the tiller so that the rudder helped to clear enough depth in which the blades could function. 'Hope we don't meet anything,' she muttered. Then, as she throttled down to neutral in a particularly sticky place, the engine cut right out. As we turned the starting handle again . . . and again . . . and again . . . we cursed the

Georges, we cursed the idiots who had sent us out with an obsolete engine and we cursed the engine itself.

'Perhaps it will start if we let it cool off,' suggested Virginia.

So we stopped there in the middle of the narrow channel, indifferent and impervious to the possibility of other boats wanting to pass. An hour later we tried again but, apart from a hesitant cough, there was no response so we gave up and abandoned any hope of moving to a more convenient stopping place. In the morning I would have to phone yet again for help, and the thought plummeted me again into depths of gloom.

The next morning I primed the engine as usual without any feeling of hope that it would start. Yet such was the cussedness of that wretched engine that it did start on our first half-hearted swings on the starting handle!

'Whatever happens, don't let it stop until we tie up tonight,' I said.

We soon realized that it was in the neutral position that the engine was most likely to cut. When changing straight through to reverse there was no problem but the neutral position remained a constant threat so that we learned to keep an eye on the shafting in the cabin and, if it kept turning, however slowly, the solid thump of the engine was maintained.

We continued our slow progress to Claydon hoping that our troubles were in abeyance. All went well until the Cetus stuck firm on the cill of the bottom lock. Although we pulled with a line from the mast and flushed down as much water as we dared, the boat remained stuck in the mouth of the lock. Then a lock-keeper appeared and rashly – as we thought – opened both sluices to lift the boat clear, but the pound at the top of the locks was reduced to a thin trickle between banks of brown mud. We made clucking noises about the water levels and the need for a really efficient pumping system but the lock-keeper remained unruffled and laughed at our concern.

'Got you through all right, didn't we? Probably get a good storm before you come through again.'

'I wonder if he'd have been so friendly if *we* had emptied the pound,' commented Virginia as we waved our farewells.

Then there were the swing bridges! On the Grand Union there had been only one, at Winkwell, an easy bridge to move and, with one of the crew on the towpath to open it for the oncoming boats, there was no need barely to throttle down. We were taken unawares on that first trip by the constant appearance of yet another bridge looming ominously ahead. The liftbridges are a feature of the Oxford, and how attractive they look in photographs and brochures. Now, they are mostly kept open, secured into position by chains and padlocks, but forty years ago they were in use by farmers as regular footpaths so that they were always in the 'down' position.

'Bridge ahead,' was bellowed by the steerer directly the familiar obstacle across the canal was spotted. Either Virginia or I would jump off and race ahead to get the bridge into the open position so that the boats could continue without being checked – we were always so fearful of that engine cutting out. The bridge, once opened, was then anchored by Virginia or myself sitting as heavily as possible on one of the arms. There were moments when we shifted to get a more secure purchase on the beam that the bridge would waver to incur fearful jerks of panic at thoughts of boat and crew being guillotined by the descending drawbridge. (The rickety old liftbridge in Banbury was still as precarious when daughter Helen and I make a trip back in 1974 to re-savour the delights of the Oxford. It still shivered with imminent threat of collapse each time it clanged back into position and we lowered it as gently as one would treat a very old lady – no doubt that, in later years, I have begun to identify with its frailty!)

The Python was at Aynho wharf with his load of coal still intact but no one was around. I thought I saw a corner of the lace curtain over the porthole move slightly as we passed and, as the chimney smoke was in full spate, I guessed that the steerer was in the cabin.

For much of the way we had glimpses of the River Cherwell as it wound alongside the route of the canal. Then, through Baker's lock we found that we had left the safe, if occasionally tedious, confines of the canal and were travelling on the deep water of the river itself. As in the dock basin our loaded boats seemed very small and vulnerable with that depth of water beneath them and the few inches of freeboard above the waterline very inadequate to keep the cargo and ourselves from submergence in the dark waters below. But how the boats swam on the short stretch of 'real' water before we had to turn off again through the diamond-shaped lock back into the canal as it continued its way to Thrupp and down to Oxford. If only that lovely, deep river could have taken us all the way, we said, how much quicker and easier our trips would have been!

We came to the waterlilies at Thrupp. There was only the slightest indication of a channel through them and, as we hilariously floated through this water-garden of flowers, we pulled up the long trailing stems to make garlands for the 'ellums and the tillers. How they stank! Now, the lilies have retreated to the muddy shallows under the trees and there is a wide channel between them and a long line of moored boats along the towpath side; but they *are* still there, and so too is the right-angled bend slap through one of the liftbridges which still has to be raised when boats are passing. (When we were on the Alphons there were plenty of strong-armed men around all too willing to flex their muscles and to smile encouragingly upon the old girl at the tiller. A few surprised nods of approval too followed as the boat swung round the sharp bend, responding immediately to the judicious extra swish on the tiller so that it fitted neatly through the narrow gap under the bridge. Once learned, it seemed, the old skills remain – a comforting thought as I remembered some of the hazards the Oxford had in store for the unwary.)

That first trip with the Hercules and the Cetus was by far the most exhausting. The engine of the Hercules was never dependable and we were still learning to work together as a crew. We had no idea where shops were to be found, and on that first trip we went right through Lower Heyford without realizing there was a sizeable village behind the wooded banks. Now, the problem of tying up is that of space rather than of time and depth of water. Shops are frequent and shopkeepers welcoming to passing cruisers and their crews. In past days of emergency ration cards we were often met with suspicion and refusal. A bargee (as we were wrongly named) was never quite respectable, whatever the accent!

On that first trip we did not even go into Oxford. The boats were offloaded almost immediately so that there was no excuse for delay. As we had surmised, the return trip with empty boats posed no problems, and the tedium of the trip down with the loaded boats was almost forgotten in our enjoyment of that lovely countryside in full summer. Virginia and I made ourselves black skirts – shortened versions of those worn by many of the boatwomen – from black-out material she had brought from home, and with our boots and wide leather belts we must have looked as if we really 'belonged' to the boats and the canals. Helen was more reserved and conservative in dress as in her whole attitude to the boats and I never remember seeing her in anything but trousers even on the hottest of days.

At Banbury we met up with Bert Tooley, who told us that Christian and her crew had left the boats, so I phoned Mr Barlow to ensure that we could take over Hyperion on our return to Hawkesbury three days later.

11. *Hyperion*

30 June
I moved my small store of belongings from my bug-infested cabin on the
Hercules. The Hyperion is a joy – easy to start and with a steady,
confident note to the engine. No leaks and no bugs!

The exchange of the old Hercules for the Hyperion signified a real
change from the almost continual record of difficulties and disasters to more sporadic recording of incidents spaced out over the
following months which indicates that, for most of the time, we
delivered our loads of coal with *almost* monotonous regularity.

With the Hyperion we reverted once more to the two-hourly
shifts which had been abandoned over the difficulties with
Hercules. We had taken on coal at Longford, and Helen took the ·
motor while I was on the butty to give Virginia time to clean up
the cabin – and Candy! – after the invasion of the coaldust.

'Watch the bilge pump,' I said as she took over and I stepped off
in a bridge'ole to get aboard the butty.

All was blissfully quiet and enjoyable on the long, straight
stretches of the top Oxford.

'Cocoa,' said Virginia. 'Just enough hot water left for a
couple of mugs. Helen can have hers when we change over at
Hillmorton.'

The steaming cocoa was welcome, and Virginia came out to sit on the side of the well-deck for a brief respite from the cleaning. Automatically she leaned out to look at the motor and Helen's trim back.

'Help . . . the bilges . . . HELEN,' she shouted at the top of her voice.

She was on the planks laid over the coal and onto the foredeck of the Cetus, where she continued to shout and wave her arms to attract Helen's attention. Morosely I leaned over the side to see a fine spray of oil spill through the open doors of the engine-room – open to show off all our cleaning and polishing efforts while we had waited to be loaded! I shoved the tiller hard over to put the butty on the mud, hoping that Helen would turn round when she felt the pull on the snubber (we had begged a new one from George, taking full advantage of his sympathy for us over the raw deal we had experienced with the Hercules).

She turned . . . and immediately saw what had happened. In a panic she put the engine hard astern. Luckily Virginia on the foredeck was able to pull up the soft length of sisal before it caught round the blades.

'Neutral . . . neutral . . .' we both yelled as the oily murk spilled out even more fiercely. Helen wound the gearwheel feverishly until the engine died into neutral and the butty drifted slowly up towards it.

'Stop the engine,' I called. Had it been the Hercules, the engine would have cut of its own accord! To stop the Hyperion's engine one of us would have to descend into the engine-room to cut off the fuel supply.

'Give me that piece of cleaning rag,' Virginia shouted to me.

She tied the far-from-clean polishing rag over her head, scrambled onto the motor counter and along the gunwale and backed down into the engine-room.

Helen went through a pantomime of abject remorse which had me laughing despite myself. After all it was my fault as well. I had intended to watch the outlet as I knew that often one or other of the pumps tended to get blocked after coaling. Thankfully the engine stopped and Virginia leaned out, dungarees and head 'scarf' and face liberally splashed with oil blots.

'Dreadful,' she said wearily.

'Sorry, my fault,' Helen and I both said together – then laughed. The tension was eased – that's how it was, and the reason that we *were* such a good crew despite the differences between us.

The filthy oil was everywhere. Both pumps were blocked with grit; it had been a crass oversight on my part not to have checked them before we started, or at least not to have watched for the outlet. We had learned another lesson the hard way. There followed the dreary task of emptying the bilges with tin and bucket until the level was again below the flywheel and we were able to re-start the engine to pump out the rest. We heated Cut water in a large preserving pan I'd bought cheaply from a junk shop in Coventry and cleaned off as best we could. The familiar thump of an approaching boat disturbed our labours.

'Hell, it's Kit.' I recognized the trim figure standing on the gunwale – a constant perch through the long hours of instructing for both trainers.

'Trouble?' she shouted.

'Bilge pump,' I shouted back with a grimace.

Kit made a face to express sympathy and vexation. Her attention was riveted on the new trainee at the tiller, who was neurotic about edging past us. Their empty boats were not so easy to manoeuvre in the narrow space and with the light breeze blowing them towards us.

'Have a good trip,' Kit called facetiously as they cleared us and continued on their way.

Finally we too were able to continue, thankful at least for the ease and reliability of Hyperion's engine. We progressed smoothly and without further incident, all of us with concentration and attentiveness fully stretched. There *had* to be no more mishaps, or none that were due to our lack of competence.

There was to be a temporary reversal in the saga of our mishaps and misdeeds as, during this trip, we were able to *give* assistance rather than always to be in need of it.

16 July
Bill Humphries' mule in Cut below King's Sutton lock. We managed to get it out but it was very lame. Left it at farm above Aynho to be collected on return. Towed the Humphries to Oxford.
20 July
Still working three boats on return trip. Collected mule from farm but it still seems very feeble.

Working three boats through single locks was a tedious business, and then we had to tie up at the bottom of Claydon as the locks were padlocked at 6 p.m. The Humphries were anxious to continue independently, and they had left by 5 a.m., before we were up: '23 June. *Left bottom of Claydon at 5.45 a.m. No sign of the Humphries. Butty 'ellum off in short second lock.'*

The three full-length boats in procession round some of those bends must have been a sight which would have filled the most experienced of pleasure-craft owners with apprehension. Even my present boat, the Alphons, was regarded with suspicion and anxiety on our recent trip round some of those bends. 'Shouldn't allow such big boats on this stretch,' said one such owner as he leapt ashore to hold in his cruiser with a couple of lines to give us a wide berth. I wished I could have reincarnated the progress of the three boats for his benefit!

When we thought of Bill Humphries' mule and the thin-shanked mares sweating and straining at the overloaded timber barges, we were reluctantly grateful for diesel power. When we watched the Skinners' boat gliding easily and silently along the muddy pounds, we thought 'How idyllic!' The horse-drawn barges, like the gipsy caravans with the piebald ponies tied on behind have always evoked a kind of magic and a nostalgic regret for their passing.

Not so long ago I was sitting in the cabin of the Alphons late on a summer evening. The boat was tied up on the towpath side somewhere along the Tring summit. The slap of a line on the cabin roof startled me into an awareness that someone was outside, and further slaps as the line moved along the length of the cabin roof and the soft thuds of a horse's plod transported me in memory to past days on the working boats. The smell of horse came in through the open window, and the unmistakable shape of horse legs came into my line of vision. When Joe Skinner's horse and Bill Humphries' mule worked, it was considered both unwise and inconsiderate to tie up on the towpath side except in an emergency. A stationary boat could foul the line – and the Alphons was tied on the towpath side! This horse obviously had someone to lead him, someone who had expertly flicked the line clear of the chimney and the water jugs. I rushed out to the fore-end to see who could be passing – and what a sight met my eyes. A boat was sliding past, the open hold sheltered by a striped awning. There were lights and soft music and I waved madly at the faces turned to look at me. On the bank a magnificent horse was being led by a young girl, who with a last deft flick cleared the cratch of the Alphons.

'Sorry,' I called after her; the girl turned and waved. Did she realize that I was in the wrong, I wondered, as the boat receded into the darkness.

I was never wholly convinced of the superiority of the motor over the horse, especially after a trip round the Lower Road or after loading at Griff or Newdigate when the role of barge horse was forced upon us. We were faced with eleven uphill locks at Atherstone with loaded boats, and while one of us went ahead with the motor, the other two bowhauled the butty up through the locks. It was a hard start at the end of a busy coaling day and not helped by covert comments and jeers from the German prisoners of war on the bridge spanning the Cut which took them from factory to their camp behind the high stone walls. It's likely that the comments were of admiration and surprise – even today the sight of two young women in dungarees and boots pulling a loaded boat through a stretch of locks would evoke comments of surprise and some incredulity – but we were always convinced that the remarks were disparaging! They were Germans, after all, and the propaganda was very effective. Also we had seen those carcases of meat being taken into their camp when we had been unable to obtain any meat on our emergency ration cards!

We were always thankful to reach the top and to return to more human – even feminine – occupations such as shopping and bathing. The trainers had done their best to make contacts along the route where we might avail ourselves of a bathroom but the typewritten list of such amenities (still inserted into my diary) is discouraging rather than helpful.

Landladies at Blue Lias and Two Boars – offer what facilities there are – no bathrooms and no water laid on.

Warwick – lock-keeper's wife in Cape district willing to offer what facilities she can – no bathroom.

Buckby Wharf – Mrs Dawson of the New Inn – no bathroom. She will not make any charge except for use of towels . . .

There was also a kind lady in Leighton Buzzard who offered us the use of her spotless bathroom. Unfortunately we were always so dirty that the thought of leaving muddy footprints on her carpeting deterred us from taking advantage of her kind offer. For most of the time we depended on the utilitarian public baths in Coventry and Oxford.

We continued our trips down the Oxford through the long summer days and into the autumn, taking our loads of coal to the papermills at Wolvercote, to Steveco, Morrells and Osberton Radiators. We had come to know the twists, the liftbridges, the stepping-off places, the more helpful shopkeepers, the best tying-up places and of course the pubs. The George and Dragon, the Wise Alderman and the Pigeons were among the many pubs where we found hospitality and welcome breaks back into civilization at the end of a day. One of our favourite ties was at the Pigeons, a one-roomed tavern right alongside the canal with a great tree in front, which had a seat built all the way around it. There were only ever one or two locals who found their way to drink there, and it was a mecca to us, so that we always tried to arrive there during the barely defined opening hours. Sadly, it is no longer there; a nice, suburban-looking house marks the spot. When I was last there on the Alphons, a rickety lock gate which delayed our progress somewhat obscured my romantic memories. The usual strong-armed men appeared from nowhere to offer advice and to unwedge us from the ill-fitting gate. No one remembered the old pub except one woman who was living on a converted Josher at the top of the lock. Waves of friendship passed between the two old women who shared such memories!

Another of our favourite stopping places was at Nell's Bridge near Somerton. A kindly farmer's wife had befriended us and she used to prepare a box for us containing a chicken and vegetables all ready prepared for cooking. If possible we tried to be there on a Sunday as the locks were often closed through the dry season for the one day a week. The chicken dinner demanded my undivided attention as the range so quickly rushed to extremes of temperature unless a constant vigil was kept upon fuel and dampers. I couldn't recognize the farm now as the short stretch above the lock is crammed with boats, and the farm is obviously more profitable as a hire-boat centre.

Very occasionally on the long, hot days of that summer working down to Oxford, if the water was reasonably deep and clear where we happened to be tied, if there was time enough and *if* we had the necessary energy, Virginia and I would go for a swim in bras and pants. More often we combined the pleasure of a cold bath with the continuous inspection of the shafting. Almost always it was fouled by wire, lengths of old rope and the soft, sodden remnants of sacks and clothing. Half submerged and with feet drawn up to keep clear of the mud, we hacked and cut away the clogging debris after which we felt we had earned our liberating swim.

I asked Vi once if she ever went swimming in the Cut and she looked at me with horror. 'None of us can swim,' she replied. 'Don't reckon to fall in either.'

Traditionally the locks have always been used as swimming-pools by the more venturesome lads of the locality. The added attraction of forbidden territory (there used to be notices at certain points that unauthorized persons found using the canal would be fined £5) added zest to their exploits. The Watford lock was always a favourite rendezvous for the local gang and, as women, we were fair game for their dares of bravado.

During that August we had orders to deliver coal to a factory on the main line. At Fenney we had been glad to stock up with the tins of milk – cocoa tasted so much better with evaporated! And at Watford lock there were the lads waiting for us. They dived off the side just as we were navigating the boats into the lock, while others, still on the bank, shouted. 'Watch out, Missus – man overboard – you've 'it 'im – 'e'll drown,' going through a pantomime of exaggerated gestures to delay our progress and to keep our attention away from working the boats. How well they succeeded! Those lads were expert at diving right down under the boats so that we were in mortal fear of having to rescue crushed corpses. They survived like corks only to laugh at our fears and to hang on to every available handhold on the boats. We entered the lock with bodies draped like fenders along the sides, then, one by one, they dropped off at the last second of safety as the boats entered the narrow confines of the lock gates. There were never any adults around to deter their enthusiasm and we soon realized that their judgements of safety were infinitely superior to our own. Shining and shivering, with snotty noses and water-streaked hair, they clambered over the gates to shut them behind the boats.

'Let's 'ave yer iron, Miss. We'll wind like we do for the proper boaters.'

'Not allowed,' I said as Virginia and I wound up the paddles as efficiently as we knew how under the stream of their good-natured and ribald comments.

'See you on return,' they shouted as we moved slowly out from the lock still accompanied by the flotilla of white bodies until they tired and returned to their swimming-pool to await the next pair of boats.

VJ Day passed with only a brief mention in the logbook we kept at the time: *'15–16 August. Peace day celebrations. Waiting at the depot for repairs to be done.'* The repairs to the engine could hardly have been of any significance as no further reference is made to them.

Virginia was in greater need of attention and 'repairs' than the engine. Her hair had become infected with lice; we thought she might have caught them from a fair we visited in Leighton. Helen cut off all her hair and then soaked her poor head in a solution of paraffin! We were due for a week's leave, so she and Candy went home for beauty treatments, and I went back to my base in Chelsea. Helen had already left on an extended leave.

The entries in my diary record brief references to concerts, dances, parties and people. What energy! I try to recall the faces of those who have become to me just names in the diary. Who was M.F., I wonder? Apparently he took me to dinner at L'Ecu d'Or! And then I read, *'Very thankful to escape and return to the quiet remoteness of the boats.'*

There was yet another load of iron pilings to be taken from the top of Norwood back up to Tyseley before returning to the coalfields and the Oxford run. Virginia and I worked well together and decided we could manage two-handed for the trip north. I had phoned Helen and she would join us at Coventry. We made our way in and out of Brummagem in the early hours to avoid the fun-and-games of the idle young which were rather more unpleasant than the diving games of the youngsters at the Watford lock. Faces would appear over the parapet of a bridge as we approached and we'd take a piece of coal from the heap in readiness on the cabin top. We were entirely vulnerable to their well-directed spumes of spit and even their well-aimed stones.

They knew we couldn't get off the boats fast enough to catch them and they had all the unfair advantage of protection from our aims behind the parapet. Some of the boatmen kept catapults at the ready and used them with good effect. In later years we followed their example as the threats from the vantage points on bridges in the poorer districts of the cities increased rather than diminished.

A photograph slips out from the back of my diary (*see* Pl. 6), and I am reminded that Freddie, a journalist friend of mine, came for a brief visit to the boats during our previous trip down the Grand Union. He joined us at Coventry, hoping to do a write-up for one of the magazines. Poor Freddie, he hadn't much time to do any writing! He was kept fully occupied with steering the butty as Virginia was unwell with an attack of jaundice. I remember we put him to sleep on one of the topsheets on the coal under the cratch! As I look at the photo, I remember the incident well. The butty with Virginia aboard had been loosed off and had slid neatly into the shallow stop lock at Hawkesbury (*see* Pl. 12) with just the right speed and at the right angle. I had felt justly proud of my good judgement, especially as there was an audience of boatmen waiting for orders by Mr Vieter's office – now the sanitary station! Helen is leaning cheerfully on the shaft pretending to be doing something useful. I had indulged in a little showing off and circled the Hercules round the narrow confines of the small basin. This had involved 'three-point' turns, executed with what I imagined to be an easy nonchalance, and I had been rewarded by the barely distinguishable nods and comments of approval. I pulled up neatly outside the Greyhound, bought the milk which I see in the photo is on the cabin top and was offered a pint and a sandwich by one of the men. I felt I was one of them at last!

Freddie gallantly stayed with us as far as Leighton, where he took a photo of us as we tied up.

Visitors came and went – and we were always glad when they went! The extra body was always in the wrong place at the wrong time, an immovable object which often blocked the necessary manipulations with ropes and tillers. 'Sit on the cabin roof,' one of us would suggest. Then, 'Mind while I jump . . . Stand on the gunwale . . . No, come back into the hatches . . . You'll get swept off . . . Perhaps it would be better if you walked along the towpath while we're locking . . .' Politeness to one's friends was always a great strain!

The trips down the Oxford continued through the autumn. We took a few days' leave at the end of every three trips, and often we 'rested' for the few days at Oxford, from which it was easier for Helen and Virginia to travel home. I was more than content to stay in charge of the boats with time to browse around the bookshops and to visit the Playhouse. I remember seeing Eleanor Bron and Rosalie Crutchley still in the early days of their careers.

Our routine was well established and the incidents recorded in such profusion during our first trips together dwindled into more personal commentaries and speculations about the state of my life, the society in which I had lived before the boats, opportunities lost and speculations about the future.

Just one other incident is recorded during those autumn days. I had bought a chimney from Charity Dock at Bedworth, resplendent with brass fittings: '*20 October. The new chimney was swept off under the willows. Retaining chain wrenched and broken. Collected one of the plain variety from Bert Tooley on return trip.*'

The loss of a chimney overboard – especially a decorated one – was a near tragedy. We wasted a lot of valuable time fishing for it with the shaft but the bubbles had vanished by the time we had dealt with the boats and got the shaft into action; the chimney was lost for ever in its muddy grave under the trees.

Not only did I have to forgo my cabin fire throughout the working day but the loss of protection which the chimney afforded was disturbing. On Sunday mornings when the water was good, the locks were kept open and we had to keep on the move. Through the autumn the towpath was lined for miles with silent and unsmiling anglers. We knew they resented the boats which disturbed the peace of their meditations; the old feud between boatmen and fishermen was all too evident. With the width of the canal often no more than twenty or thirty feet, our progress resembled that of a wedding procession – possibly a funeral procession would be more apt – as we passed through an archway of fishing lines which lifted in vertical salutes to our advance and fell again in sequence when we had passed. We felt embarrassed at this interruption to their fishing and at the close proximity of scowls and impassive hostility, so that, like all boatmen, we kept the chimney firmly positioned between us and the buddhas on the bank. How grateful we were to collect a replacement from Bert Tooley so that I could keep my fire going and feel once more that I could slouch in the shelter of its protection!

Thirty years later on the Alphons we suffered a similar mishap. 'Those willows,' I thought as we eased our way down the muddy channel. A cruiser approached from the opposite direction and I eased right down so that the boats could slide past each other without either of us being forced into the side. But the steerer of the oncoming boat panicked and at the last moment revved instead of slowing. Too late I revved the Alphons; the wash from the cruiser flushed our boat over to the branches of the waiting willows, where a sharp, cut-off branch lifted the bicycle neatly from the cabin top and dropped it into the water. By the time I had brought the boat back into the channel there were only a few bubbles to indicate where the bicycle had vanished so quickly. My raucous shout brought my daughter Helen from the cabin; she was in the water at once, the stern rope in her hand – she has been well trained to cope with such emergencies! Luckily she located the precious bike with her feet and hitched the rope around the handlebars so that, between us, we were able to drag it back on board, covered with thick mud and minus the pump but otherwise none the worse for its immersion.

That trip we called on Bert Tooley, who was still working away in his well-stocked shed by Banbury lock. We talked of boats, past and present, of prices and of people. He remembered Christian and myself (and Virginia's dog!), along with the Skinners, the Cresswells, the Brays, the Humphries and others, many dead now and their families dispersed and merged into alien and 'established' patterns of living so different from the lives of their parents and grandparents on the boats.

At the end of October 1945 Helen left the boats for good and we were joined by Pat. She was serious and over-conscientious and we missed the gay hilarity of Helen's idiotic duckwalk along the towpath when she tried to rally our drooping spirits at the end of a long day. We missed too her light, inconsequential attitude to the work and to our more serious striving for perfection. She used to come and meet us in Oxford when possible and she was doubly welcome, for herself and also for the home-made cakes and the eggs she brought us – remembering our insatiable appetites!

Pat stayed with us through the gloom of November. She had been away from the boats for some time and was adamant in her refusal to steer the motor. Secretly I think Virginia and I were relieved, as we were both competent steerers by this time and knew how to avoid most of the hazards. To both of us Pat was a godsend. She loved cleaning and polishing; she kept the butty cabin spotless and orderly, and even Candy obeyed her ruling that she was to sleep in a box at the back end of the cabin and not on either of the beds. She was tireless at lockwheeling and was happy enough to steer the butty on the straight stretches. It all worked out very well despite the change in our cherished routine. But she stayed with us for only a couple of trips as she had problems of her own to cope with at home.

So Virginia and I continued to work two-handed and learned to pace ourselves and the work so that we never endured the extremes of exhaustion we had suffered in the early days. We each enjoyed the luxury of a cabin to ourselves, and our free time in Oxford was far more enjoyable than free time in either Brummagem or Southall. The only drawback was the lack of news and contacts from the other trainees on the Main Line. On our trip south back in early September we had met up very briefly with Daphne and Olga. Daphne had told us that the gossip of the time was that Sonia was to marry George. Speculations about the union were lively and sanguine and we half envied her the superior status of mate to a real boatman!

Then, late in November when we were tied at Hawkesbury, Mr Vieter told us that Kit had left and that Audrey and Daphne would be leaving after their next trip. The news was unsettling and we began to wonder how long we would continue to be employed by either Mr Barlow or the GUCCC.

The weather had been reasonably mild, although early in December there was a brief spell of frost and fog, a reminder of the ice-up of almost a year ago. One evening we tied up at Noble (Newbould), and on 6 December, '*We were visited by David from Rugby who cycled over to find us. Then George and Sonia tied up alongside and came round to see us. All of us piled into the butty cabin. Much talking – Sonia has great plans for the amelioration of the boatpeople's conditions. Everyone has left already.*'

Later in the month Mr Barlow arranged for us to pick up a load of pilings from Bull's Bridge so that we would be back at the depot for Christmas. Virginia planned to stay with friends as her mother was in South Africa. I decided to stay on board, where I felt more at home than in my bed-sit or with friends from whom I felt increasingly estranged.

We were loaded and tied at the top end of the wharf just outside the paint shop so that we would be ready to start immediately Virginia returned. Before she left we sheeted up and coiled ropes and topstrings in the proper manner; we used a lot of elbow-grease on the brass and felt justly proud of all our efforts. Candy stayed in the cabin, scared of the rough-looking mongrels on the bank. Virginia had decided to leave her with the friends as Candy would have to be mated. Somehow I found it hard to imagine Virginia without her dog! When they had both left, my cabin strangely felt too quiet and too empty. There were no other trainee crews there; I was told at the office that most had left as boats were queuing up for the dwindling number of orders. We had heard only rumours of the situation on our regular coal runs down the Oxford, and I felt uneasy when confronted with the reality back at the depot.

I walked down the length of the lay-by to see if there was anyone else I knew. Most of the boats were empty, and their cratches rose high up out of the water like dolphins. The line of the upturned butty tillers etched the sky like beckoning arms, and smoke from the cabin chimneys rose straight into the windless air like loosely held scarves flicked by the beckoning arms. The boats were end-on to the wharf, and it was so warm that most of the cabin doors were open. It was tempting to stare into the light and the warmth but instead I looked away and walked purposefully as if I had business at the far end. I saw no one, although, later, several had seen me!

The next morning Virginia returned saying that plans had gone awry. 'You know how it is,' she said by way of explanation and I knew indeed. Already we seemed not to belong to the conventional routine and comforts we had exchanged for our present way of life, which had little to do with old standards, old ambitions and old values. She had left Candy behind to be groomed for motherhood. Her absence on the boats was another gap in our crew which threatened our permanency. Helen, then Pat and now Candy. I knew that Virginia was still under pressure to resume her studies and I wondered how much longer she would be able to hold out. I wondered too about myself and whether I would ever be able to return to teaching, shut into the restrictions of authority and routine, the constant demands of pupils and the claustrophobic enclosures of a school. My old headmistress had tried to persuade me to get re-admitted into the career structure but the idea of returning to such constrictions appalled me. Marriage too seemed to offer only similar restraints and limitations upon the freedom I had found in my life on the boats.

Meanwhile it was Christmas again, and on Christmas Morning there was a service in the schoolroom. Virginia and I decided not to go, as we still felt 'outsiders', more so since we had been working away from the main stream of the boats. We felt rather deflated, disappointed that none of the other women trainees was there. Then Lil Smith called around and invited us for a cup of tea with her mum and dad and younger brothers and sisters. We felt very honoured and drank tea from lovely china cups and saucers. Lil could read and write, as she had stayed with an aunt in Braunston for several years and gone to school there. She had a copy of Dickens' *Christmas Carol* and read a passage from it to all of us. We had saved up our sweet coupons and had bought literally thousands of 'hundreds-and-thousands' which we put into coloured paper twists for the children. Eli Nixon's tribe also received their share as they followed us along the wharf and waited hopefully on the bank by the Smiths' boats. We always had a soft spot for them – there were so many of them!

The next day we were off before light, but even then we heard two other pairs loose off before us. We set off quietly, subdued by a prescience of the end.

181

12. Endings and Beginnings

'Why did you leave the canals?' is almost as common a question as 'Why did you become a bargee?' and, against the backdrop of the current scene when a pair of working boats has become an object of historical interest, it's a question I've often asked myself.

Solitary 'singles' and working pairs have become the focus of idle curiosity, anomalies in the crowded scene of the pleasure craft and, as such, are not considered viable as serious commercial enterprises. Yet these pairs keep alive a flickering hope that an enlightened Ministry will again utilize the waterways network before it is irretrievably lost, so that chains of boats will be used to relieve the pressure on roads and fuel. It is estimated that, under average conditions, a single horse can move two tons on level road, equivalent to ten tons by rail and *eighty* tons by water.

The waterways of Germany carry about one third of all the heavy freightage and present a real example of an efficient network which maintains a proper share in the transport systems of the country. During the post-war years of reconstruction in Germany, political motives were strong instigators of economic revival and development, and there can be little doubt that the waterways must have proved to be of sound economic advantage or they never would have survived. The scale in Britain is different, but does not the same principle apply? Even in 1946 the future of the canals for commercial transport seemed precarious. The docks were in a state of chaos after the bombing – but not more so than in Hamburg, Minden, Cologne and other ports of loading and discharging along the Rhine, the Mitteland canal, the Dortmund-Essen and the Weser, all of which I was to visit after leaving the narrow reaches of the Grand Union and the Oxford.

There were fewer and fewer orders for the boats from either Brentford or Commercial Road. Most of the boats were returning empty to the coalfields, and even there we often had to wait days for orders. We began to feel that to stay on was unfair to the boat-people whose livelihood depended on a constant supply of work. As in many other wartime jobs the women were only filling in the gaps until such a time as the men would return to the work they had left; we did not know at the time that so many of the young men who survived would never return to their lives on the Cut.

I left the canals unwillingly and at a time when the current scene was unforeseeable. Those six years of war were a strange interlude in our lives, and most of us *thought* of them as an interlude, a chunk out of our youth, a step sideways which would be redressed as soon as circumstances permitted. Virginia and I both talked about staying on but Virginia was being pressured to return to university; as it was, she decided to take a Government-sponsored secretarial course. After she had gone I was again at a loose end in London, having frantic regrets about leaving the boats. Nostalgically I wrote:

30 January
Back again in Chelsea. I am doing just what I imagined I'd be doing, looking back and sighing for stretches of muddy water, for the Corot willow trees, for sunsets and cabin fires. At a distance even the oily bilges, the ill-fitting nuts and bolts and the dripping stern gland become the friendly trials of a very friendly life. The Beecheys, the Cresswells and the Skinners are cursing the cold, the icy ropes and the frozen planks, wishing that they were snug in a house on shore. How they would really hate to leave their boats. How we have wished ourselves back again!

I went back to the depot at Southall to see if there was any chance of being employed to work a single motor but it was not considered safe or desirable for a woman to take a boat on her own. I must have had my own doubts about it as well as I did not pursue the matter. I had come to respect the hazards which beset even the most experienced of boatmen.

I also think that for most of the women the conditions on the boats were too exacting. The lack of basic comforts and amenities to which we had been accustomed were not so easily acceptable as a more permanent condition of our lives. So often we felt dirty, overtired and hungry. We were too accustomed to regular baths, to available shops and to a well-established pattern of living which was totally different from the unpredictable hazards of living on the boats. Then, late in 1945 'bread units' were introduced, which meant that bread, our staple diet, would now be rationed and it was hard to imagine how we would manage on a limited supply. Even worse, when any commodity was rationed, it became difficult to obtain for those who could only shop with emergency ration cards. 'For regular customers only' we used to see printed in the butchers' shops and on the tea and sugar counters. If the supply of bread was to become precarious, we felt that this added problem was insuperable.

There was no incentive to stay and it was taken for granted that now the war was over – had been for almost a year – we would return from whence we came. So the scheme of women trainees – and we were never more than 'trainees' to the boatpeople, which indicates how they ragarded us – dwindled to an end and we stepped back into our predetermined roles. There was no final celebration, no reminiscences or thoughts that we would ever return to the Cut. All the other crews had left, and we felt the desolation of being the last to go and wanted only to be gone. We disbanded as quietly and separately as we had come, a motley crew of women to whom the words 'bargees' and 'water gipsies' had a magic too strong to be resisted when the opportunity to become one of them was made possible by the event of a war.

After I left I tried to take a course in navigation as I had a notion to become a lighterman on the Thames, but the chink of opportunity had closed: no women were eligible for such courses. By leaving the boats I had shut the door behind me. There was no cause for celebration. Of all the trainees only Sonia espoused the work on the canals, but then she had also espoused George, one of the real boatmen. Her 'step sideways' had become her way of life.

13.   Thirty Years On

I sit here on the Alphons, over thirty years later, remembering
and ruminating in the darkening half-light, with past and present
fusing into a composite collage of boats and canals. Beginnings,
ends and more beginnings. The chain reaction to an impulse
those years ago has echoed through the subsequent years. Sometimes the reaction has faded almost to extinction or to memories
and fancies in the mind; sometimes the momentum has gathered
itself into more positive and purposeful action directed towards
the waterways.

Was it entirely by chance that one Easter I found myself
walking along the towpath of the Leeds-Liverpool canal? I was
new to the area and had not concerned myself with canals and
waterways for many years; other importances had claimed my
time and attention. Although we had heard of the great network
of canals north of Birmingham, I was totally unfamiliar with such
names as the Shroppie, the Macclesfield, the Caldon and the rest.
When I found myself on the towpath of the Leeds-Liverpool, I
was surprised by its width, the good state of maintenance and the
total lack of traffic.

I sat on a swing bridge above the Lydiate boat club – completely
deserted – and wondered why I didn't have a boat, any kind of a
boat – a canoe, a dinghy, an inflatable even – and I wondered too

why I hadn't thought about canals and boats for so many years. They provided such an obvious escape from the over-intensity of academic seclusion; the canal itself wound along the edges of the college sports field. I remembered seeing a stack of canoes in a padlocked shed on the campus; I would ask to borrow a couple so that the children and I could sniff around the reeds and water-meadows so near to the city and yet so remote.

I sat on the swing bridge for a long time. I tried to open it; it was stiff and heavy but it responded to my efforts. I had succeeded in getting it halfway open and it was beginning to swing nicely when a car drew up and an angry driver leaned out.

'What the hell are you doing? Where's your boat?' he yelled. His indignation was justified! I had opened the bridge on another of those unpremeditated impulses and I had enjoyed the moments of concerted muscular effort to get the bridge swinging. The motorist continued to protest as I vainly tried to stop the bridge before it clanged into the open position. His scorn was even more evident as my efforts to pull the bridge into action again proved ineffectual. Why wouldn't the bloody thing move? I dug in my heels, clenched fingers round the iron staple and heaved with every ounce of my 150 pounds. I jerked at it and suddenly it moved – too easily! I looked up and the driver, a balding elderly gentleman, was casually pushing against the gate rail. Obviously he knew his bridge better than I did!

'Sorry,' I managed to blurt out of my ignominy.

'It always starts better from this end,' he said briefly. He got into his car while I pretended to make sure the catch was fastened.

He leaned out of the window as he went. 'Don't play around with the bridges on this stretch,' he admonished. 'You could be fined for tampering with Waterways' property,' and he drove over the wooden bridge and across a track on the far side.

I felt suitably humiliated. A woman in her fifties playing around with swing bridges! At that moment I decided to be once again a legitimate user of swing bridges. However small and insignificant my boat, I would still have prior rights over motorists to open a bridge for the passage of my boat! I remembered a hump-backed bridge on my way to Ormskirk and a fleeting glimpse of boats lining the narrow length of water. I drove straight there; it was the Burscough boat club I had seen. A jovial character in yachting cap and guernsey welcomed me in through the wire-netted fence. I wanted a boat? He summed me up with a glance and took me along the line of craft to an eggshell-blue 'noddy' boat.

'A real lady's boat,' he said. 'Nice and clean. Ready to drive off.'

I flinched at the language, but she *was* a nice little craft, a Loftus Bennett from Liverpool with good mahogany doors, transom and bulkheads on a fibreglass hull. The cabin had four bunks and there was a small but adequate galley area. I had visions of weekends and holidays exploring the extensive northern network. He sent me off to the owner, a young girl about to move away from home to work in Portsmouth. She was in a hurry to do a deal and I got the Karianne for £350.

She *was* a nice little boat except for that confounded steering wheel and the wire cables which invariably snapped or stretched in awkward or inopportune situations. Also it offended my boatwoman's sense of rightness to use the engine as a rudder! It was reasonably efficient except in a wind, when the whole cockleshell made little or no response to cables or to outboard steerage; we went with the wind or else crabwise or not at all! But on the good days we had fun.

We had many enjoyable holidays on the Karianne, although I looked with envy at the imposing length and the easy pace of the 'narrows' while their steerers ignored my 'noddy' as a nonentity which had intruded into their rightful territory. I kept to my place in the shallows by the banks as they drifted effortlessly by. I remembered with nostalgia the Hyperion and the Cetus; if only I could have conjured them from the past into a reality of the present, how those steerers would have envied us – at least on our better days! To work a pair of boats is still the ultimate ambition of most young canal enthusiasts, little knowing how the trainee women would have envied the comforts and conveniences that a restored boatman's cabin can offer. As my family and I chugged along in my little blue 'noddy', I little thought then that once again I would be sitting in such a cabin aboard the Alphons which has become our home.

I think with affection of the old Karianne. I think of the time we took the little boat right up through the Pennines in company with a similar boat from Lydiate. Our friends owned a small

187

portable television set and together we watched the first landing on the moon. We were high up beyond Gargrave and, to me, the landing on the moon was no more of a miracle than the building of that canal right up and through the steep gradients in the centre of England at a time when all the work was done by gangs of navvies with picks and shovels.

I kept a logbook then, as always, and am reminded of another holiday along the lovely lengths of the Shroppie and of a particular incident which triggered off my dormant responses as a boatwoman. We had come to the Audlem locks, with my son, Giles, steering and myself on the towpath to lift a paddle and to open the bottom gates of the empty locks. We were going up and an elegant Anglo-Welsh hire-boat was coming down. An energetic young woman came down the towpath waving a windlass at me.

'Leave the lock,' she shouted, 'We're just two locks above.'

I was somewhat at a loss to know what she meant as the lock we were about to enter and the next one up were both empty and ready for the Karianne to proceed. The hire-boat also had two locks to negotiate and we would pass on the longer pound between. The Karianne came into the lock and I closed the gates behind it. The young woman protested, 'I told you we were coming down.' I explained that we would make the locks ready for her boat and that the boats would pass each other easily in the pound above the next lock. She seemed to accept the logic of my explanation but then returned to the empty lock above and started to lift a paddle at the further end in order to fill it. I wound up the paddles on the lock we were in – nice easy ones – and raced up to stop her. Luckily she was new at the job and was still struggling to lift the first paddle. I told her that she would waste a lockful of water but she had her own ideas and, after all, I was only an old woman.

'I have to get the lock ready.' She spoke very slowly, as if to my idiot child.

My old anger flared immediately and I gave my windlass a whirl. 'You draw a paddle and I'll report you,' I shouted. I had little idea to whom I would report and afterwards thought how stupid my complaint would sound. 'She drew off a lock against me,' sounds like a feeble accusation to any but those to whom water conservation is a religion. I must have looked fierce as she

188

hesitated. The Karianne had now risen and was nosing through the open gate.

'Open those gates,' shouted Giles from the well. The Anglo-Welsh was now in the lock beyond but there was still plenty of time for us to be through the empty one ahead.

'You'll hold us up,' said the young woman but made no further effort to lift the paddle I had dropped. The crew on her boat must have worked feverishly in their efforts to reach the empty lock before us. As the Karianne slid into the chamber, the Anglo-Welsh, bristling with heads, appeared at the top. Bodies leapt off with ropes and a deal of shouting as I closed the bottom gates and hurried to the paddles. I'd show them how to be efficient even though we were only a 'noddy' crew. A youthful male, his naked white skin looking vulnerable in the hot sun, demonstrated his virility by whipping up the paddle to wash the poor Karianne about like a cork in the millstream. I scowled and kept my windlass on the other paddle to wind up when the turbulence had ceased.

'I'll wind it up for you,' he said.

'Bloody well leave it alone,' I shouted. 'You'd soon swamp the boat at the rate you're going . . .'

'Been out long?' he asked – inadvisably.

'Been at it all my life,' I snarled; and at that moment I was Lil, I was Vi, I was Rosie, I was one of the real boatwomen to whom the canals belonged and these were interlopers who needed to be put in their place.

There have been so many times when well-intentioned young men have given me the benefit of their advice and their muscles. More often than not it is easier to pander to their arrogance and to abrogate my own, but their presumption always irritates me.

'Always leave a boatman to work his own boats. Never touch a rope unless you're asked.' These are maxims which continue to stick firmly in my small store of the unwritten codes of conduct. The reason for these two 'rules' soon becomes obvious to the more habitual frequenter of boats: the boatman has his own particular way of working, knows precisely what he's about and will ask – or shout – for help if and when required. A helper, however well-intentioned, will mostly confuse and bungle an otherwise co-ordinated and controlled manœuvre.

I bring the Alphons in alongside – wind permitting – easily and comfortably in my own way. I take in the bows, then go astern with the tiller hard over so that the boat straightens up. I step off from the counter with checking-strap and short shaft. If the bows swing outwards, I have the shaft ready to hook the front strap into my reach. How often has the strap from the bows been grabbed as I approach the bank and turns taken round a stump to halt the boat abruptly so that the bows crash and the stern swings out into the channel to leave me marooned on the counter cursing the idiot who has bungled my well-timed exercise. Even worse, the fatuous comment, 'Brought her in a bit fast, didn't you?' leaves me speechless – although not always! I am then left to haul myself onto the cabin roof to shaft the stern back from the opposite bank only to realize that the idiot has tied the rope so tightly that the boat cannot be moved. It so often happens that other boats begin to appear from both directions and there is the Alphons strung across the Cut blocking the channel. I have to clamber along to the fore-end – the idiot strategically has disappeared – to loosen the tie and then return to shaft the stern so that, finally the boat is alongside at least ten minutes later than was necessary.

'A woman driver . . . what do you expect? Crazy to be in charge of such a big boat . . .' The feeling of helpless rage against all the stupid, ignorant, well-meaning gongoozlers and amateurs who force me into such predicaments leaves me boorish and ill-tempered for the rest of the day!

I equally resent the brashness of those who jump onto my boat without permission – often without necessity, those who scrape along the hull of my boat with their hire craft; those who peer in through the windows; those who let their untrained dogs loose regardless of any other dog, cat or canary on another's boat; those who throw their litter overboard or leave it to rot in large plastic bags along the towpath; in fact, I begin to resent all those who have usurped our way of life on the canals without bothering to inform themselves of the simple rules of conduct which have controlled and eased this nomadic and independent way of living and working.

The canals are now bristling with marinas and every kind of pleasure craft. Will the structure of the canals survive the onslaught? The question looms constantly in meetings, magazine

articles and news bulletins. I am pessimistic. The action ma-
chinery grinds too slowly to combat the erosion, the battered
gates and the rapidly increasing pollution. While groups of real
enthusiasts dig and work to recover some of the lost, derelict
stretches, the regular roads are silting up with the channel
washed away by the churning speed of highly powered craft
which are hardly suited to canal travelling. The banks are crumb-
ling faster than costly and sporadic efforts at piling can shore up
the eroded underhangs; the leaks and loss of water is greater than
that replaced by the infrequent pumping stations. Side-ponds,
whose use was enforced by the vigilant lock-keeprs, are now
dried up and full of weeds. When control finally is exercised, it
could well be too late.

Can I end on such a dreary, pessimistic note? I look out of the
window and, involuntarily, a sigh escapes me. Already there are
signs of activity in the boatyard – preparations for the coming
season. Boats are being divested of their canvas shrouds; engines
are being accelerated into bursts of noise to test their efficiency
after a winter's rest. Men in overalls are clambering with their
bags of tools in and out of the narrow hatchways, and there is a
fair sprinkling of visitors who are looking at the boats and
wandering round the workshops, some to book a holiday, others·
to make enquiries and to ensure that all the 'mod.cons.' are
available for their camping holiday. Another season is about to
erupt into the peaceful scene of the waterways.

I have no place here. I am an anachronism, a relic from the days
when boatpeople treated the Cut with as much care and respect
as if they had built it themselves. They had to, of course. No water
in the pounds, broken lock gates and collapsing banks meant
stoppages,loads delayed, contracts lost.

I return to the last entries in my old diary and look at the
scrappily kept logbook, old letters and a more comprehensive
logbook of recent travelling on the canals. I look at the letters,
brown at the creases, which are tucked away in the back of my
1944–5 diary. One is from Daphne back in Cork refitting her
boat the Embla, and she writes that Olga was with her persuading
her to join in a smuggling campaign to bring in brandy, laces and
perfume from France (it never materialized). The other letter is
from the late Tommy Rolt written from Athlone in Eire and dated
12 August 1946, when they were exploring the Irish canals. He

writes that, 'The Grand Canal is a most efficient organization which handles considerable traffic and would give us points in many respects.'

I look at the two letters, and vague thoughts about leaving my life on the Alphons surface and crystallize into a purposeful decision. Daphne is still very much alive and active and we have maintained a sporadic correspondence through the years. She has had to give up her sailing days on the Embla and now lives in County Wicklow. I shall go to visit her, and if we are too old to work a boat, we can still walk the towpaths and explore the less frequented reaches of the canals where problems of restoration and usage have not, as yet, seriously arisen. And we can talk!

Author's Postscript

I sold the Alphons in 1984, and it felt like an act of treason. But I knew that life on the canals was no longer safe for an elderly, lone woman like myself. I went to Ireland, stayed there and bought a ruined cottage in West Cork. Daphne and I have talked for long hours and walked along the towpath by the Grand Canal at Naas and Tullamore, where the old, picturesque pleasure barges still make their daily trips through the summer. She has read a great deal of this script, as much of it concerns herself. It seems like a tidy end to a lifelong love-affair with boats and waterways.

M.C.

Glossary

Bowhaul	To pull a boat along manually with a rope from the bows, or more often from the mast, to the bowhauler on the towpath (*see* p. 96).
Breasting up	Tying the two boats at bows and stern so that they lie side by side. Often used when travelling with empty boats so that only one member of the crew was needed to steer. Also used on entering locks with loaded boats in certain situations (*see* p. 67).
Bridge'ole	The channel under a bridge narrowed by the width of the towpath so that the water was deeper and the boats close to the bank to allow for exchange of crew between the boats and to prod the shafting for accumulated detritus when it impaired progress. Black smoke from the engine exhaust was a certain indication that old rope, sacking, wire, bedsprings even was fouling the blades (propeller) and/or the narrow lengths of shafting between the blades and the stern of the boat. A bridge'ole was also the most convenient place to step off – with or without

	the bicycle – for lockwheeling or shopping.
Butty boat	The non-powered boat towed by the motor boat. 'Butty' derived from 'buddy' or mate.
BWB	British Waterways Board.
Checking Strap	Rope attached to the back end of the butty for checking the boat on entering a lock.
Cill	A stone platform at one end of the floor of a lock – to be avoided in a downhill lock when the boats could catch on its edge unless kept well forward. It was used for inspection of the lock gates and also by boatpeople in certain situations (*see* p. 41).
Cotton line	Ropes of varying thicknesses used for tying the boats together – as in breasting up – for mooring and for cratch decoration. The top strings holding the topsheets in place were usually of cotton. Cotton ropes were soft and pliable, yet very strong. Well scrubbed they kept very white and the coils on the cratch strings added to a boat's smart appearance.
Counter	The rounded stern end of the motor boat.
Cratch	A triangular structure at the fore-end of a boat. It supported the top planks and was often sheeted up into a tent-like structure which protected a cargo of coal from the in-flow of water in an uphill lock. Under it we stored the large top sheets when not in use and it was even used as a spare 'bedroom' (*see* p. 176).
'ellum	Corruption of helm – the top half of the great wooden rudder on a butty boat into which the curved wooden tiller was slotted. It was often decorated with a plaited rope design known as the turk's head and occasionally a horse's tail – relic of earlier times – was affixed so that it hung down behind the 'ellum.
Foredeck	The flat, rounded area at the front of each boat between the cratch and the stem, about four feet in length. A heavy metal hatch cover

	protected a small area underneath in which were stored spare ropes, the snubber when not in use, wood, and odds and ends.
Freeboard	The few inches on a loaded boat between the deck counter on the motor and the water level.
GUCCC	Grand Union Canal Carrying Company.
Gunwale	A narrow ledge – four inches wide – on the motor boat from the counter along the length of the cabin to the hold, allowing access to the engine-room through the side-doors – often necessary for the steerer to make quick checks on pumps and charging etc, whilst on the move! It also provided a useful perch for the trainer with a new trainee under instruction. On my converted boat, the Alphons I kept a gunwale to run the whole length of the boat to make for easy stepping off and on (*see* plate 17).
Joshers	Boats which once belonged to Fellows, Morton & Clayton Ltd. – named after Joshua, one of the owners.
Pound	A stretch of water between locks – referred to on rivers as reaches.
Quant pole	The name refers to a long, pointed pole used for punting on rivers and on the Broads. On the canals such a pole had a metal pointed and pronged end and was always known as a shaft pole.
Shaft poles	Wooden poles with forked metal ends used for pushing boats away from the bank or off the mud (p. 38) for clearing rubbish accumulated in locks, and for a great variety of other uses. We carried two such shafts on the boats, the short shaft – about 10' long was always kept on the cabin roof of the motor ready for use and the long shaft, about 15' long was kept in the hold of the butty – often threaded through the top strings of the stretched sidecloths and also ready for action.

196

Snubber	A towing rope used on long pounds with loaded boats – a boat's length long and made of soft sisal. When not in use it was stowed under the foredeck of the butty.
Stern gland	The aperture in the stern of the motor boat through which the shafting from the engine to the propeller passes. The gland was packed with yellow tow to prevent seepage into the cabin bilge.
Straps	A general term used for ropes.
Strings	*Side strings* – thin ropes attached to the sidecloths for tying up and over the top planks keeping the sidecloths (attached to the sides of each boat) in a tautened stretch to protect a cargo of coal.
	Top strings. These were thicker lines (or ropes) which kept the heavy top sheets in position. There were three of these which formed a tent-like structure over the top planks and over the sidecloths and were used to protect more general cargo from the docks.
Swan's neck	The curved steel helm on the motor boat. The detachable tiller – usually brass – slotted over the reduced ambit of the helm and was held in place by a tiller pin (often the top end of a brass poker) slotted through the tiller and the helm.
Tipcats	Round rope fenders on the back end of the motor boat. Probably so called after a game played with the round fender used as a ball.
Well-deck	On the butty boat the deck area from which the boat was steered was partially enclosed by sides of approximately three feet in height from the floor of the deck. This afforded protection for children of the boating families.
Winding hole	(pronounced as in kindling) An enlargement

	in the width of the canal to allow for turning a full length boat (72').
Windlass	Sometimes called a 'key' or 'iron' by the boatpeople. It is a metal crank handle to wind the lifting gear of the sluices in a lock gate.
Woolwich	A type of boat built for the Grand Union Canal Carrying Company by Harland & Wolff Ltd. Our boats were small Woolwiches.

Further Reading

Alsop, R & Dodkins, G. *Working Boats*. 1988.
Bird, Vivian. *By Lock and Pound*. 1988.
Blagrove, David. *Bread upon the Waters*. 1984.
Cornish, Margaret. *Still Waters*. 1982.
Foxon, Tom. *Anderton for Orders*. 1988.
Gayford, Eily. *The Amateur Boatwomen*. 1973.
Hadfield, Charles. *British Canals*. 7th edn, 1984.
Lewery, A J. *Narrow Boat Painting*. 1974, reprinted.
Liley, John. *Journeys of the Swan*. 1971.
Mackersey, Ian. *Tom Rolt & the Cressy Years*. 1984, reprinted 1991.
McKnight, Hugh. *The Shell Book of Inland Waterways*. 1976, reprinted.
Malet, Hugh. *Voyage in a Bowler Hat*. 1960, reprinted 1985.
Paget-Tomlinson, Edward. *The Illustrated History of Canal and River Navigations*. 1993.
Rolt, L T C. *Narrow Boat*. 1944, reprinted.
Seymour, J. *Voyage into England*. 1966.
Smith, Emma. *Maidens' Trip*. 1948, reprinted 1993.
Stewart, Sheila. *Ramlin Rose: the boatwoman's story*. 1993.
Wilkinson, Tim. *Hold On a Minute*. 1965, reprinted 1990.
Woolfitt, Susan. *Idle Women*. 1947, reprinted 1986.

Index

People are listed alphabetically by first name

201

—CANAL COINS—

STANLEY HOLLAND, the first to tackle this subject in depth, covers the whole range of British canal numismatics (tokens, medallions, ferry tickets, etc), and includes a sample of foreign waterway coins and medals. To tempt the collector further, he looks at the related subject of Britain's official canal badges and buttons. A full check list of British tokens and medallions is appended.   ISBN: 0 947712 18 5

—THE CANAL BUILDERS—

This classic, by ANTHONY BURTON, deals at length with the birth of the canals: their planning, promotion, engineering and building. Our new edition incorporates the results of latest research, and a useful bibliography on canal engineering.   ISBN: 0 947712 21 6

—THOMAS TELFORD'S—
—TEMPTATION—

For years, the great canal historian CHARLES HADFIELD was puzzled by the fact that Telford's autobiography makes little mention of William Jessop, Telford's senior on both the Ellesmere and Caledonian Canals. His masterly pursuit of the explanation reads like a detective story.   ISBN: 0 947712 19 4

—L.T.C. ROLT: a bibliography—

IAN ROGERSON and GORDON MAXIM have compiled a useful catalogue of the writings of the 20th century's most important industrial historian. Over 300 items of Rolt's published work (books, booklets, reviews, articles etc.) are listed and indexed.   ISBN: 0 947712 04 6

—*The Working Waterways series*—

In this series, we have captured the fascinating details of what it was actually like to work on England's canals in the 1940s, 50s and 60s. Every book in the series has been written by a man or woman who actually worked narrow boats, and the whole thus provides an authentic record of a vanished scene.

—*The Historical Canal Map series*—

A series of well-researched maps showing, for the whole of England and Wales, all the waterways ever built or authorised by Act of Parliament.

—*The Waterways Heritage series*—

Facsimile reproductions of important canal documents from the past, accompanied by explanatory notes.

—THE HUT SIX STORY—

No-one else but GORDON WELCHMAN has written a personal account of working at Bletchley Park (Britain's WW2 codebreaking centre) throughout the war. This is both authentic and important.   ISBN 0 947712 34 8

—TOP SECRET ULTRA—

PETER CALVOCORESSI presents this valuable account of his work as an RAF Intelligence Officer at Bletchley Park (Britain's WW2 codebreaking centre) 1940-45, providing an authoritative overview.   ISBN 0 947712 41 0

—MY ROAD TO BLETCHLEY PARK—

DOREEN LUKE describes her war work as a Wireless Operator/Morse Slip Reader, ending up at Bletchley Park for the last three years of the war.   ISBN 0 947712 44 5

—DOC KEEN AND THE BOMBE—

The first published account of how a brilliant engineer, Harold Keen, worked with the great Alan Turing to create the 'Bombe' - a unique and unprecedented code-breaking machine which helped Bletchley Park to crack the German Enigma codes, and thus win the war. Harold's son, JOHN KEEN, has compiled this biography of his father.   ISBN 0 947712 42 9